PRAISE FOR *VALIANT WOMEN OF THE BIBLE, VOLUME 1: FROM EVE TO ESTHER*

Valiant Women of the Bible, Vol. One: From Eve to Esther by Laura Zielke is a masterful work that highlights the often-overlooked stories of women in the Bible. Zielke's meticulous scholarship and ability to uncover hidden details bring these biblical women to life in a way that is both empowering and inspiring. Her storytelling is vibrant and engaging, ensuring that these women's potential is fully realized and celebrated. The book is a delightful blend of insight, humor, and wit, making it an enjoyable read while offering profound lessons. This is an essential read for women seeking a modern understanding of classical biblical narratives to enrich their lives.

— Dr. Jenny Rain
    Author, Speaker, & Founder
    Jenny Rain Coaching

This book is the book I didn't know I needed. Rarely do we get to take a deep dive into the women named in the Bible and their stories. Valiant Women of the Bible does just that - not with the typical, cursory glances, but with purposeful mastery that illuminates intentional God-markers in their stories. I tried to ask myself if one woman stood out most, but each story touched my heart differently.

Laura takes the reader through an exploratory journey in this book. I truly felt like a treasure hunter following the breadcrumbs she gave. The additional features make this book capture and keep your attention as you engage with the content. I learned more about these women than I expected as someone quite familiar with scripture. I was challenged on a personal and spiritual level, asking myself questions about my own womanhood and the truths I believe about myself. The space for reflection after learning about each woman really helps with this.

In our current societal climate, womanhood, identity, and gender are taboo and often polarizing topics. But we cannot ignore them as members of the body of Christ and as citizens of this earth called to steward our time and relationships well. This book will be an essential, yet palatable tool in starting and guiding conversations that can help heal where harm has been caused. We get to see the heart of God for women in a new and enlightening way and maybe see His heart for us individually as well.

— Quantrilla Ard, PhD
    Writer, Speaker, & Grief Coach
    The PhD Mamma/The QDL Group

Valiant Women of the Bible, Volume One: From Eve to Esther *is a captivating look at women in the Hebrew Bible. Those who are part of the Christian faith refer to this portion of the Bible as the Old Testament. Zielke immediately grabs our attention with the colorful and playful format of the book, but do not let the youthful look fool you. It contains Biblical truths, thought-provoking reflections, and historical insights validated by the Word and biblical scholars. The author's passion for responsible biblical teaching pours through.*

Zielke purposely utilizes diverse images of the women, to challenge our Western view of the Bible. Indeed, the Bible is full of multi-ethnic people. Her portrayal forces us to reconsider our perceptions. What I love most about the book is as you read, it ignites you to dig deeper into the Bible and reminds us how fun it is to study God's Word. That's what it's all about, the importance of reading the Bible and making connections: text-to-self, text-to-text, and text-to-world. This book is amazing. I highly recommend it!

— Dr. Paula C. Perez
   Author, Educator, Speaker, Coach
   DrP & Me, LLC (YANAcoaching)

Valiant Women of the Bible *was a great read. It is such an empowering and inspiring book. The insights and historical context allowed me to see these women weren't just wives, handmaidens, servants, and slaves, they were change-makers. Some of my favorites are Ruth, Naomi, Rahab, and Esther. These women are truthfully presented as powerful, forward-thinking leaders of their time. Regardless of their history or life's current situation, they all stepped into the powerful attributes God placed in them from birth.*

This is a well-thought-out and researched book. I loved the Digging Deeper sections which are a bible study on their own. The modern images and writings are captivating. It makes you want to keep reading. I felt pulled into every story as they represented the lives of many women today. Valiant Woman of the Bible provides encouragement and empowerment for women today. It doesn't matter your history, circumstances, or lifestyle, God has a powerful plan and purpose for your life that He will fulfill as he orders your steps.

— Judy A. Mott-Butler
   Owner/CEO
   Christian Moms Prosper

Valiant Women of the Bible *by Laura Zielke is enlightening and well-researched. Throughout Zielke's book, I was encouraged to dig deeper, share my findings, and help others make connections. Learning about Sheerah, the city builder, was especially impactful—her story was completely new to me. I was aware of the concept of "cities of refuge," but not of one being built by a woman. That idea challenged my perception of gender roles in architecture and city planning in the ancient world. It caused me to reflect on how I teach my students to perceive gender roles in jobs today. I plan to use this excellent resource in the mission field, especially with ESL learners.*

— Rev. Kevin J. Pope
   Missionary
   Ulsan English Fellowship, South Korea

The story of Hagar deeply resonated with me as a divorced, single mother raising a son and striving for the best for him. Feeling alone and often caught in a difficult relationship with his father, I found Zielke's insights into Hagar's story, drawn from word studies and ancient texts, to be profoundly personal and spiritually uplifting. Discovering that Hagar is the only person in the Bible who names God—and calls Him El-Roi, "the God who sees me"—was mind-blowing! This realization gave me hope, spiritual comfort, and a sense of relief. It reminded me that God also sees me in this challenging time of transition and that, like Hagar, I am under God's protection and care.

As a two-time seminarian, I was thrilled to see the critical discourse around ancient biblical languages and the inclusion of scholarly references from highly respected experts, as well as archaeological insights. What impressed me most is how Laura presents these complex topics in a way that's accessible and engaging for everyday readers. The book is scholarly, entertaining, enriching, and easy to understand. I also appreciated the questions for reflection and suggested actions at the end of each chapter, which make it a practical resource for personal and group study.

This book will bring healing to many women. It would make an excellent study resource for churches and ministries, especially for those looking to connect more deeply with the courageous women of the Hebrew Bible and foster fresh, meaningful dialogue with the women in their lives.

— Rev. Countess Cooper
   United Church of Christ Minister
   and USAF NG Military Chaplain

The stories and interpretations presented in this book are based on extensive research and the author's perspectives. While every effort has been made to ensure accuracy, some historical and cultural details may be subject to interpretation. This book is intended for informational and educational purposes only and should not be taken as a definitive historical account. Readers are encouraged to consult additional sources and engage in their own study of the biblical texts. Errata may be requested by writing to the above address or viewed online at https://valiantwomenofthebible.com/errata.

Library of Congress Control Number: 2024912865

Zielke, Laura, 1967- author.
    Valiant women of the bible, volume 1: from Eve to Esther / Laura L. Zielke. — First edition. 2024.
    p. cm.
    ISBN 979-8-9904354-1-4 (paperback; standard paper)
    Includes bibliographical references and end notes.

    1. Women in the Bible. 2. Biblical history and archaeology. 3. Old Testament studies. I. Title.

10 9 8 7 6 5 4 3 2

VALIANT WOMEN OF THE BIBLE

Exploring the Lives, Courage, & Achievements of Women in Bible Times
VOLUME ONE: FROM EVE TO ESTHER

For too long, women in the Bible have been viewed as supporting characters in stories about men.

This stops now.

In *Valiant Women of the Bible, Vol. One: From Eve to Esther,* you will learn the stories of twenty-two remarkable women from the Hebrew Bible through a fresh, culturally informed, and historically grounded lens. Each woman is brought to life through the use of modern photos, engaging narratives, sacred imagination, and archaeological insights.

When you read this book with a curious mind and fact-check it with your Bible, you might uncover new perspectives and rethink traditional interpretations based on what the text actually says. You'll be inspired to dig deeper and truly appreciate the impact these strong women had on their families, communities, and nation—especially considering their religious, cultural, and socio-economic status in the ancient Near East.

Let's grab our metaphorical shovels, dig in to the Scriptures, and witness how the actions of a few courageous women shaped the biblical narrative and paved the way for the promised Messiah.

VALIANT

OF THE BIBLE

Exploring the Lives, Courage, & Achievements of Women in Bible Times
VOLUME ONE: FROM EVE TO ESTHER

Written by

LAURA L. ZIELKE

Published by A2Z Marketing — A Division of My Living Tapestry, LLC — Sanford, North Carolina

For Mom

Thank you for raising me to stay curious and ask questions. You are a valiant woman who has modeled a life of service and dedication to the Lord. I've witnessed you regularly step out of your comfort zone to follow God's prompting—impacting many lives in the process. Every morning, you start your day with a cup of coffee and your Bible, taking time to read, reflect, and pray. From there, you move into your roles as a caregiver and friend, always offering your love and support. You are wise and brave and strong. I'm so thankful God gave me you as my mom.

And Dad

Thank you for working so hard as a pastor to build strong communities of faith filled with people who love God, love people, and love the Word. More than college or seminary, I learned the most about the Bible from you. Week after week, verse by verse, phrase by phrase, you showed me how to love, read, study, and teach the Bible in an accessible way. And thanks for not going easy on me when we'd play Bible 20 Questions. I'll never forget your stumping me with Jesus' feeding of the 4,000! I'm so thankful God gave me you as my dad.

TABLE OF CONTENTS

Valiant

MORE PRECIOUS

"A woman of strength [valor] who can find?
She is far more precious than jewels."
Proverbs 31:10

VALIANT

/'val-yənt/

Adjective:

1. Possessing or acting with bravery or boldness: COURAGEOUS

2. Marked by, exhibiting, or carried out with courage or determination: HEROIC[1]

Valiant

Welcome, Valued Reader!

This book is a labor of love, crafted with you in mind. I wrote it to illuminate the incredible women and girls named in the Bible whose stories deserve to be told. Understanding our past not only enriches our present but also inspires our future.

This project began during Women's History Month in 2017. Out of all the posts and articles about amazing women jamming my social media feed, **none** of them were about women in the Bible. And as a Bible nerd, this was not okay with me.

So, the next year, I decided to write and share brief posts about the women whose stories I knew. The title for the project came to me right away: *Valiant Women of the Bible*. In fact, I recently found a post from early 2019 where I shared the title with a group of writer friends!

The title is based on Proverbs 31:10 which says, "A woman of valor, who can find?" Zalman Goldstein and Chaim Fogelman offer this translation (and a bonus insight!) in their article on *Chabad.org*:

> Eshet Chayil (or Aishes Chayil or אשת חיל) means "woman of valor." It is from chapter 31 of Proverbs, which praises the woman. Each line begins with another letter of the Hebrew Alphabet.[2]

I eventually turned the social posts into an email sequence and made the subscription available year-round. The response from my subscribers was both encouraging and eye-opening.

Readers loved learning about the different women, but many were surprised by their stories. I'd get emails with comments like, *"Wow, I'd never heard of her before!"* and *"I've been a Christian for 40+ years and didn't know about this woman!"* and *"How did I not know this?"* The feedback really impacted me and pushed me to do more to bring these stories to a wider audience.

Therefore, I took a deeper dive into the Bible, conducted more research, dug into the original languages, prayed hard, and then rewrote every story, painting a more vibrant and historically grounded picture of each woman's life. I have done my best to honor the God-breathed inspiration of the Bible and "rightly divide the Word of Truth" (2 Timothy 2:15).

The result is a two-volume series entitled *Valiant Women of the Bible*. Volume One (this book) features the biographies of more than twenty women* named in the Hebrew Bible.** The forthcoming second volume includes biographies of (at least) fourteen women in the New Testament.

To bring these stories to life in a way that is both engaging and respectful, I've embraced what Dr. Wilda C. Gafney refers to as "sanctified imagination," a creative approach detailed in her book *Womanist Midrash*:

> Sanctified imagination is deeply rooted in biblical piety that respects the Scriptures as the word of God and takes them seriously and authoritatively...The sanctified imagination is the fertile creative space where the preacher-interpreter enters the text, particularly the spaces in the text, and fills them out with missing details: names, back stories, detailed descriptions of the scene and characters, and so on. Like classical and contemporary Jewish midrash, the sacred imagination tells the story behind the story, the story between the lines on the page.[3]

Filling in the gaps does not change the core message or meaning of a passage, and it's not adding to God's Word—this is not Scripture. Instead, this approach slows us down enough to appreciate the nuance and what might have been happening behind the scenes. So, regardless of where we find our valiant woman, we know she was doing the best she could at the

---

*These narratives are not just for women; they are for anyone interested in the profound impact of these women throughout biblical history. My aim is to honor their stories in the most inclusive and respectful way possible, contributing to a broader understanding and appreciation of their roles in our spiritual heritage. Although the title and focus of this book adheres to the traditional binary and focuses on the lives of those assigned 'female' at birth, my intent is not to make a statement about sex or gender identity, but rather to celebrate the strength and resilience of these historically marginalized humans. I invite readers of all backgrounds and identities to find inspiration in their stories.

** Following a valuable discussion with a Jewish friend, I've chosen to use the term "Hebrew Bible" instead of "Old Testament" in this book. She explained that the latter term is seen as pejorative within the Jewish community, and it's important to me that this work respects the sensitivities of all faith traditions. While I acknowledge that the names of books, people, and places in the Bible originate from Hebrew—with distinct spellings and pronunciations reflecting their deep historical and cultural roots—I have chosen to use the spellings from Christian Bible translations to aid recognition among my readers. This approach aims to balance familiarity with respect for the Scripture's Hebrew origins.

time. Whether she is in the garden conversing with a serpent, in a tent changing diapers, or on the threshing floor proposing marriage, whether she's at the royal palace saving a life, on her knees begging God for a child, or putting her life on the line to save her people—each woman we encounter has her own unique story to tell.

In *Valiant Women of the Bible, Volume One: From Eve to Esther*, you will meet a variety of women who were fiercely courageous in the face of real danger, surprisingly resilient despite societal constraints, and genuinely devoted to a God they could not see, but *Who could see them*.

For the sake of clarity and narrative flow, each woman will be presented in the same order she appears in the Hebrew Bible and in history. This means that by the time you've finished reading this book, not only will you have learned about a variety of valiant women, you will also have increased your familiarity with these core events in Israel's history:

- Origin of 12 Tribes of Israel
- Liberation from Egypt
- Conquest of Canaan
- Theocracy and Judges
- United Monarchy
- Divided Monarchy
- Fall of Northern Kingdom
- Fall of Southern Kingdom
- Babylonian Exile
- Life in the Jewish Diaspora

Since I might use terms and address resources unfamiliar to you, I've taken painstaking efforts to make sure they are defined and documented, in case you'd like to learn more on your own. (*Check out the extensive bibliography.*)

Finally, the "Personal Reflection" questions at the end of each chapter are designed to help you connect what you're reading to your life. You will be encouraged to identify the admirable attributes of the woman or women in each chapter, and then discern those same qualities in a woman you know. You might be surprised how similar the challenges they faced back then are, at the core, the same ones we face today. Someone should create a Venn Diagram! 😉🔴🔵

My prayer is that this book creates a wave of encouragement, support, and empowerment that ripples across the globe as we join hands to uplift the women around us, building stronger communities through shared stories of faith and resilience. God is still working through women to bring healing to the world. I hope exploring the lives of these biblical women is as enlightening, enriching, and empowering for you as writing about them was for me. ❤️

Laura

Laura Zielke

TIPS FOR GETTING THE MOST OUT OF YOUR JOURNEY

Welcome to a journey of exploration and discovery focused on the lives of women named in the Hebrew Bible. This book comes equipped with visual cues and sidebars to enrich your understanding and enhance your connection to the Bible. Here's a guide to help you get the most out of this experience. 🧡

LET MODERN IMAGES INSPIRE YOU

Every photo and image in this book was intentionally selected by the author to spark your imagination and visually capture the essence of each story, bridging thousands of years and connecting you with the narrative. Photos of women were chosen to highlight the ethnic diversity in the Bible and to decenter whiteness. The guiding question for chapter cover photos was, "What might she have looked like had she lived during our lifetime?"

EXPLORE "DIGGING DEEPER" ARTICLES

Rather than interrupt the narrative flow, you'll find "Digging Deeper" articles on separate pages with this background photo of a woman digging into the earth. These supplemental essays feature relevant word studies; evidence from sources outside the Bible; exposition of challenging passages; theological insights; and techniques for responsible Bible interpretation. They are packed with extra information about the people living in the land of ancient Israel.

"Side Notes" are featured in pale gold boxes and anchored to the edge of the page. They contain definitions, explanations, and interesting tidbits to enrich your knowledge of the Bible and best practices for responsible biblical interpretation.

 ## REFLECT ON THE SPOTLIGHTS

The titles of spotlight articles are flanked by flashlights. These sections offer insights from archaeology, exploration of difficult topics, and thought-provoking theories to supplement what's being explored in the narrative. They will broaden your perspective with a rich and grounded exploration of the Bible.

CONTEMPLATE "SOAPBOX MOMENTS" AND "THINGS TO THINK ABOUT"

When you see the soap box or the brain, you're invited to pause and reflect. In Soapbox Moments sections, I share strong opinions and challenge common assumptions about Bible stories. Drawing on my education and personal experiences, I aim to clear up misconceptions and encourage responsible Bible interpretation. When you see "Something to Think About," it's time to slow down and take a closer look at the text in the Bible. What do you notice?

SOMETHING TO THINK ABOUT

SOAP BOX

REFER TO THE TIMELINES, FAMILY TREES, AND MAPS

Simplified timelines, historical narratives, family trees, and period-specific maps are included to help you navigate and connect the dots between the stories you're reading and the broader context of Israel's history. These tools ensure you maintain a clear understanding of how and when individual events fit within the larger historical landscape.

ENGAGE WITH PERSONAL REFLECTIONS

At the conclusion of each chapter, you'll find questions for personal reflection and optional calls to action. These are designed to help you internalize the story's relevance and encourage others in meaningful ways.

You'll see emojis sprinkled throughout the book. Because. Emojis are life!

Remember, this journey we're about to take together is not simply reading another book. This interactive experience is designed to help you engage with, reflect on, and connect to the women of the Bible in new and exciting ways.

Stay open and enjoy the journey!

QUESTIONS TO STRENGTHEN YOUR STUDY OF THE BIBLE

1. What does the text **actually** say?

2. What does the text NOT say?

3. Look at the language. Is the masculine plural being used? And if so, does this indicate women are included? (This is often the case.)

4. Who was the intended audience of the writer(s)? How should that impact my interpretation?

5. What was going on at that time in Israel's history? World history?

6. Do my resources and commentaries include diverse voices from various publishers?

7. What is the simplest understanding that aligns with what I know to be true about God?

8. It's important to remember that ancient Hebrew, Greek, and Aramaic manuscripts did **not** include any of the following:

   - Chapter numbers,
   - Verse numbers,
   - Subheadings,
   - Punctuation marks,
   - Quotation marks, or
   - Red letters.

   Therefore, have I looked at the passage embedded in its original context? What do the verses before and/or after it contribute to its meaning? The chapters before/after? It's physical location in the Bible?

9. Have I turned down the volume of the loud, obnoxious voice in my head. What does the still, small voice say?

10. Have I read the passage in 3-5 different translations? Have I read all the relevant footnotes?

11. Does my understanding align with the rest of Scripture? If not, why?

12. Am I willing to hold off teaching this passage or insight until I'm clear?

Eve

EZER KENEGDO

"Then the Lord God said, 'It is not good that the man should be alone; I will make him a helper fit for him.'"
Genesis 2:18

Eve

The first woman named in the Hebrew Bible is Eve. Her name means "life," which seems appropriate since it's through her body the first human baby is born.

Though some people view Eve's story as myth, many insist that she was indeed the very first woman—created by God's own hand. Eve's story can be divided into four sections which correspond with the first chapters of *Genesis*:

- ❖ Chapter 1 - Image Bearer
- ❖ Chapter 2 - Suitable Helper
- ❖ Chapter 3 - Rule Breaker
- ❖ Chapter 4 - Mother of All

Let's dig in!

CHAPTER 1: IMAGE BEARER

In the first creation story (Genesis 1), God creates everything from nothing in six days and rests on the seventh. Humanity is created on the sixth day.

So God created man
in his own image,
in the image of God
created he him;
male and female
created he them.
Genesis 1:27, KJV

So God created humans
in his image,
in the image of God
he created them;
male and female
he created them.
Genesis 1:27, NRSV

⏸ It's important that we **pause** here to take in the full weight of this event.

When we start at the very beginning—a very good place to start—it becomes clear that **humanity is completely distinct from the rest of creation** due to its unique relationship with the Creator. As expressed in the notes on this verse in the *New Jerusalem Bible*:

> This relationship with God marks off [separates] human beings from the animals; moreover, it involves a general similarity of nature: intellect, will, authority. It paves the way for a higher revelation: the human share in the divine nature by virtue of grace.[1]

Humans, the ultimate expression of God's creativity and power, are given a unique role in creation, equal in dignity and value. God endows them with blessings and duties, urging them to be fruitful, creative, and responsible stewards of the planet. Building on this foundation, Dr. Patricia Wilson-Kastner explains that:

> Human reality is one, and human wholeness emerges from the development of the whole of humanity, without the obstacles of preconceptions and stereotypes.[2]

Her observation challenges us to reflect on the dawn of creation and the initial unity and equality we enjoyed—unaffected by the divisions, inequalities, and biases which later arise. In the beginning, humanity is a united whole.

CHAPTER 2: SUITABLE HELPER

In the second creation story (Genesis 2), we are presented with a more detailed, "zoomed-in" account which details the creation of the first two individual humans—one breath at a time.

First, God creates a human from the dust of the earth and breathes life into him. He places the man in a beautiful garden with specific instructions about what he can and cannot eat. He then starts working on a "suitable helper."

Continuing to play in the mud, God creates all animals and birds. But, alas! No suitable helper is found. This begs the question: What does "suitable helper" actually mean? What qualities is He expecting in this creature?

DIGGING DEEPER

The Hebrew word *ezer* (עֵזֶר) is almost always referring to God, His provision, support, or assistance. Below you can view a few of these occurrences where the "help" (*ezer*) mentioned is the Lord or originating from Him:

- ✣ Exodus 18:4
  Here, *ezer* reflects God's deliverance of Moses from the sword of Pharaoh, emphasizing God's role as a protector and deliverer.

- ✣ Deuteronomy 33:7, 26, 29
  In these verses, *ezer* is used to describe God's support and defense of Israel, underscoring His power and protection against enemies and in times of need.

- ✣ Psalm 20:2
  This prayer is that God would "send you help from the sanctuary," implying the *ezer* is being provided by Him.

- ✣ Psalm 33:20
  The *ezer* is portrayed as a source of hope, with God being a shield and help, reinforcing His role as a protector and supporter.

- ✣ Psalms 70:5; 115:9-11; 121:1-2; 124:8
  Throughout these Psalms, *ezer* is used to describe God's timely help and protection. This serves to remind us of His constant presence and aid in times of need.

As you can see, the term *ezer* is consistently and repeatedly used to indicate an essential partnership grounded in strength and life-extending support. THIS is the type of helper God wants for the man. How does this impact your concept of a "helper"?

IT'S TIME TO FOCUS ON THE TEXT AND GET CURIOUS.

The familiar phrase "suitable helper" is a translation of two different Hebrew words: *EZER* and *KENEGDO* which, when used together, indicate a mutual partnership with no hierarchy. Did you catch that? No hierarchy. Don't take my word for it; see for yourself.

EZER = "HELPER"

The Hebrew word for *helper* used here is *ezer* (pronounced ay'-zer), and depending on how it's used in a sentence, *ezer* is sometimes translated as *help*. It appears 21 times in the Hebrew Scriptures—twice in Genesis 2 describing the suitable helper God will create, and **17 times describing GOD** as deliverer and rescuer; a powerful support; a source of protection for His people. (*See "Digging Deeper" on opposite page.*)

Jo Saxton, author of *More than Enchanting* and *Ready to Rise*, clarifies that an *ezer* is not someone limited to a role of assistant because they're too weak to do anything greater, but rather someone who will show up and help "because they have the passion, power, and purpose to do so."[3] An *ezer* embodies qualities of strength, capacity, and courage; it's the same word used to refer to the help that God provides.

Here's a familiar passage for your reflection and consideration. Each time you see the word "help" in these verses, it's the Hebrew word *ezer*:

I lift up my eyes to the hills—from where will my HELP come?
My HELP comes from the Lord, who made heaven and earth.
Psalm 121:1-2 (emphasis mine)

Latrun Valley, Israel ~ Located 22 miles west of Jerusalem

The second human's creation as an *ezer* sends a strong message that the role envisioned for her carries immense value and significance—comparable to God's own role as an "ever present **help** in times of trouble" (Psalm 46:1). Even here, the Hebrew word translated "help" is a feminine form of *ezer*.

Now, turning our attention to the modifier '"suitable," let's explore *kenegdo*.

KENEGDO = "SUITABLE"

Although **kenegdo** (or *kenegdu*) is often translated *suitable*, the meaning of this term is more like *a perfect match*. Carolyn Custis James, author of *Half the Church: Recapturing God's Global Vision for Women*, articulates that the helper created for the first human was not merely an assistant or a subordinate, but **someone who matches him in essence and standing, a counterpart of equal value and significance.**[4]

Likewise, in his commentary on Genesis, Herbert E. Ryle emphasizes that:

> Man will find help from that which is in harmony with his own nature, and, therefore, able adequately to sympathise [sic] with him in thought and interests. It is not identity, but harmony, of character which is suggested.[5]

WHAT'S THE TAKEAWAY FROM OUR WORD STUDY OF *EZER* AND *KENEGDO*?

What we learn is that **NOTHING** on earth has the ability to adequately and fully relate to the first human **until** the second human is created. Full stop. ⬡

The creation of a second human is not an afterthought (as we know from the account in Genesis 1), but rather a purposeful act by God. I think the gap between the creation of the two humans allows enough time for the first to realize that out of all of creation, he has no match. Both creation stories underscore that **humans are created to be in relationship with one another**—without hierarchy—embodying genuine partnership.

It's crystal clear from the text that the only possible way one human could be able to reach his full potential is in relationship with another human—someone who could mirror him, engage with him intellectually, and understand his complexity. Nothing else creation is capable of this level of connection, no matter how developed they are.

What does this mean for us today? We are being invited to build our closest relationships on a foundation of mutual support, where each person is both a contributor *and* a beneficiary—equally indispensable.

By embracing this perspective, we grasp the uniqueness of the human bond and affirm the universal longing for deep, impactful relationships. It's in these person-to-person connections, we find our collective strength—not going through life alone, but flourishing within a diverse and vibrant community that reflects the inclusive, loving nature God embedded in our DNA. These connections are not limited to marriage—not everyone is married! We are all created to thrive in meaningful relationships with other humans.

How does understanding "*ezer*" and "*kenegdo*" impact your view of the creation story? Reflect on the ways this interpretation might influence your approach to relationships, valuing **mutual** support and partnership.

CHAPTER 3: RULE BREAKER

The next scene opens with the *ezer kenegdo* having a conversation with a talking serpent. They're discussing the restrictions imposed upon her, specifically regarding a certain tree in the center of the garden: the tree of the knowledge of good and evil. Apparently, she's been told that if she so much as *touches* the tree, she will die. This prohibition is being debated.

After weighing the pros and cons, she makes a decision of her own free will to taste its fruit. Then, in an unexpected plot twist, she shares it with her partner—*who just so happens to be right there at her side!* And he also ate.

SOAPBOX MOMENT

I've lost track of the number of times I uncomfortably sat through a sermon or Sunday School lesson while the male leader shared how "hot" Eve must have been. The perfect woman. Naked. "A 10." The speaker, clearing his throat quips, "Adam wakes up and exclaims, 'WHOA-man!'" Men laugh. Women squirm. Can I get a witness?

Imagining what Eve looked like is <u>NOT</u> why we have the story of Eve's creation twice recorded in Genesis—prosaically in chapter one, poetically in chapter two. When people indulge in public fantasizing about the naked woman in the garden, they are both missing the point of the story and indirectly body-shaming the women in their audience who will never be "perfect."

I think we can all agree that the creation narratives were not written for us to imagine what Adam and Eve looked like naked, right? Okay. Onward.

Now, if you are willing, I invite you to join me in temporarily setting aside centuries of theological debates about original sin, women being more gullible than men, and the kind of fruit they ate—was it a fig? pomegranate? apple?—so we can examine the text as-is.

Let's take a look at some of the details we often gloss over or skip altogether. These are the things that make me go, "Hmmmm." 🤔

DETAIL #1: GOD COMMANDS *THE MAN*

When God places the man in the garden, He gives him full access to its bounty with one exception: the tree of the knowledge of good and evil.

> The Lord God took **THE MAN** and put him in the garden of Eden to till it and keep it. And the Lord God commanded **THE MAN**,
> "**YOU** may freely eat of every tree of the garden,
> but of the tree of the knowledge of good and evil **YOU** shall not eat,
> for in the day that **YOU** eat of it **YOU** shall die."
> Genesis 2:15–17 (emphasis mine)

Note: When God instructs him not to eat from it, He is addressing only the man. How do we know this? Easy. At this time in the detailed creation account of Genesis 2, **the only human on the planet is the man.**

DETAIL #2: GOD QUESTIONS *THE MAN*

After tasting the fruit, he is confronted by God in Genesis 3:11. The question, "Have you eaten from the tree of which I commanded you not to eat?" is directed to the *man*, not the couple. God is **NOT** asking *them*, "Have y'all eaten from the tree of which I commanded y'all not to eat?" NEITHER is He addressing the woman. God is speaking directly and only to the man. How do we know this? Easy.

The "you" in this sentence is **singular**, not plural. Although this is clear in the Hebrew text, we miss it in translation. The good news is that you don't need to read Hebrew to see it with your own eyes.

Take a look at this screenshot of Genesis 3:11 from the _Hebrew Interlinear Bible_ from BibleHub.com. _(See the Side Note below for a detailed description of interlinear Bibles and how they work.)_

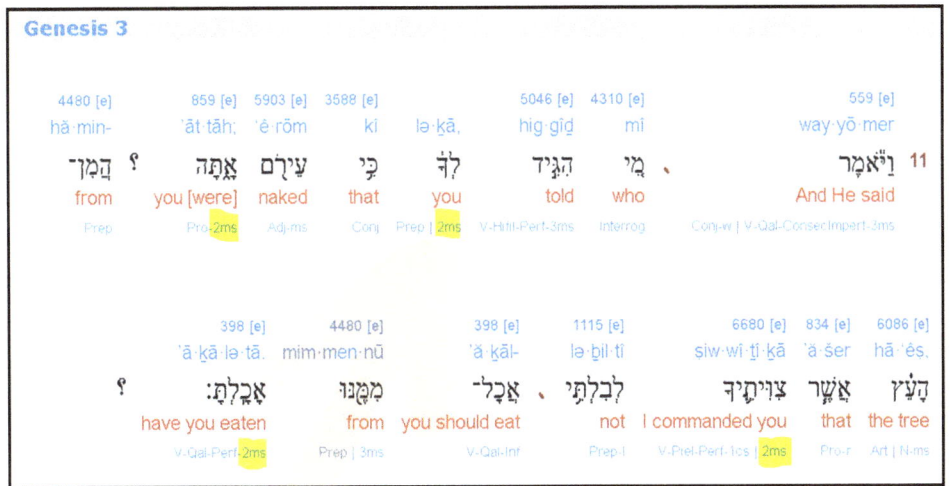

The Hebrew language offers more precise information about the person to whom God is speaking. In the image above, I've highlighted the relevant grammatical details: "2ms" indicates the word is "Second Person, Masculine, Singular."

This indicates God is speaking directly to one man:

He [God] said,
"Who told YOU that
YOU were naked?
Have YOU eaten from
the tree of which
I commanded YOU
not to eat?"
Genesis 3:11
(emphasis mine)

Side Note:
An "interlinear Bible" is an educational tool that juxtaposes the original language of the Scriptures, like Hebrew or Greek, with a literal English translation directly underneath each line of text. In the screenshot above, you can see Genesis 3:11 in Hebrew with the phonetic spelling just beneath it, followed by a direct English translation of each word. Under the English translation, there are additional notations which provide grammatical details. These include the part of speech (e.g., noun, verb, adjective), the gender (masculine, feminine, neutral), person (first, second, or third), number (singular or plural) for each term, and more! For example, the designation "Art | N-ms" indicates there's a definite **art**icle attached to this **m**asculine **s**ingular **n**oun so the translation is "the man," not "a man" or even "the men" which would have required it to be plural. These linguistic details help readers understand the text's original nuances and who is being addressed or described, resulting in a more precise translation.

Strong's Concordance Number
Transliteration (pronunciation)
Hebrew (reads right to left)
English translation (in red)
Conjugation/Parsing

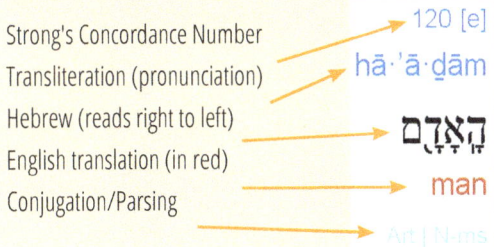

The man responds to God's inquiry by deflecting. He gets defensive and turns the attention to someone else. First, he blames God—it's *His* fault for creating the *ezer kenegdo* in the first place. 😱 Then, he blames her.

> The man said, "The woman whom YOU gave to be with me,
> she gave me fruit from the tree, and I ate."
> Genesis 3:12 (emphasis mine)

At this, God turns to the woman and asks her—wait for it—*a __completely different__ question:*

> Then the Lord God said to the woman,
> "What is this that YOU have done?"
> The woman said,
> "The serpent tricked me, and I ate."
> Genesis 3:13 (emphasis mine)

> 6213 [e]
> 'ā·śît;
>
> עָשִׂית
> you have done
> V-Qal-Perf-2fs
>
> "2fs" means second person, feminine, singular. Translated: "YOU" directed to an individual female.

The woman accuses the serpent of tricking her, and her deflection brings the themes of this story into full relief: **moral freedom** and **personal responsibility**.

As author Elaine Pagels observes in her book, *Adam, Eve, and the Serpent*:

> Its point is to show that we are all responsible for
> the choices we freely make—good or evil.[6]

In Genesis 3, the man, the woman, and the serpent are held responsible for their individual actions, and each receives a "fitting" punishment: The man is punished for disobeying God; the serpent, for deceiving the woman; and the woman, for what? What exactly did she do that was so wrong?

Her transgression wasn't engaging in conversation with a talking serpent or seeking greater wisdom. Neither was it *touching* the tree nor eating its fruit. The woman's true infraction, it seems, was offering her partner something explicitly forbidden to him by God.

The consequence? **Subjugation to her partner's authority.**

The judgment also implies that there was more going on here than a simple experiment to see what would happen if she touched the tree.

4. MOTHER OF ALL

Once the consequences have been doled out, and it's been proclaimed by God that the woman will be the one to bear children, the man finally names his *ezer kenegdo*. This marks the **first time** in the Bible where a human is given a proper name—one that carries tremendous significance:

> The man named his wife Eve because she was the mother of all living.
> Genesis 3:20

The man names her "mother of all living" even though she has yet to conceive. **Her name foreshadows her destiny**—we'll see this prophetic naming event again in the next chapter when God changes Sarai's name.

> Now the man knew his wife Eve, and she conceived and bore Cain, saying, "I have produced a man with the help of the Lord."
> Genesis 4:1

Isn't it interesting that Eve's pregnancy comes *after* God's pronouncement that her desire would be for her husband and after they are removed from the garden? In this light, Eve's story transitions from a mere account of origins to a multifaceted portrait of her identity and legacy.

A QUICK REVIEW

Who is Eve? Some view her story as an ancient myth, while others see it as an etiological tale explaining the origins of pain in childbirth. Yet, many believe Eve is, indeed, the first literal woman fashioned by the hand of God. She is the second human, the first woman, and a prototype for all women to come.

According to Genesis, Eve embodies many roles: wife, mother, grandmother, and great-grandmother. Described as a suitable helper, she is created with

---

SOMETHING TO THINK ABOUT...

When you ascribe to the doctrine of original sin, be sure to also embrace the freedom and total reset Jesus accomplished on the Cross. Why? Because whatever the Fall did, the Cross undid. The Apostle Paul articulates this in Romans 5:12-21.

a fierce independence. Characterized by curiosity, inquisitiveness, and boldness, she is persuaded by a serpent to ignore what her partner says and touch the tree of knowledge of good and evil. After touching it and not dying, she tastes its fruit and then offers it to her partner who follows her lead.

The consequences are swift and severe; however, that's not the end of her story. She and Adam get busy and before too long, they have two boys running round. We can imagine Eve's heart breaking in half when her firstborn son murders his brother—we have no idea how old the boys are when this happens.

Despite this horrible tragedy, Eve conceives again and praises God when she delivers yet another baby boy (Genesis 4:25). This is what we know for sure about Eve. Everything else is speculation.

You can read Eve's story in **Genesis 1-4**. ✴

Personal Reflections

What stood out to you?

Did reading this chapter prompt further questions?

Look at the cover photo for this chapter and imagine why it was chosen. What do you notice?

Is there someone in your life who reminds you of **Eve**—someone who is insatiably curious? Enormously brave? Always willing to try something new? Or maybe someone who has navigated a tragedy within her own family and emerged from it still praising God?

Consider sending her a quick text, encouraging message, or longer letter to let her know you're thinking of her today. Acknowledge her strength and/or share one way she inspires you to rely on God.

If the woman you thought of is you, please send a message to the author at **info@valiantwomenofthebible.com** so we can encourage you to keep on keeping on!

chapter two

Sarah

MIRACLE MOM

"God has brought laughter for me; everyone who hears will laugh
with me...Who would ever have said to Abraham that Sarah
would nurse children? Yet I have borne him a son in his old age."
Genesis 21:6-7

Sarah

Now it's time to turn our attention to one of the **MATRIARCHS** of Israel. "Matriarchs?" you ask. Yes, matriarchs. 🙌

You're probably familiar with the patriarchs: Abraham, Isaac, and Jacob. Well, I'm here to remind us all that they each were married to *at least* one woman, and each of their wives was right there alongside them taking big steps of faith and trusting God to provide direction, protection, and conception.

The matriarchs were essential to the establishment and continuation of the Israelite line. They birthed and raised the founders of the nation.

The first matriarch is Sarah; however, when we are introduced to her, she is called "Sarai" which means "my princess." She is married to a man named Abram, and they have no children (yet).

Sarai is beautiful inside and out, and she is deeply dedicated to her husband. Early in their marriage, God promises Abram an heir if he leaves everything behind—family, friends, and his homeland—to follow Him to an unspecified destination. Trusting in God's promise, they embark on this journey together.

No matter how you cut it, this is a HUGE step of faith.

The original pioneer woman and her husband have no idea what challenges lie ahead of them, but they know that together and with God's help, they will handle anything that comes their way. Sarai's loyalty to Abram shines brightly in two notable situations where she agrees to call herself his sister to protect him from potential danger due to her beauty.

The first incident occurs early in their sojourn when they migrate to Egypt due to a famine in Canaan. Sarai's beauty immediately captures the attention of pharaoh's officials; therefore, she is introduced not as Abram's wife, but as his sister (Gen. 12:10-20). This happens again years later with the King of Gerar, Abimelech (Gen. 20:1-18). Each time, Sarai executes Abram's plan perfectly to ensure his safety. She trusts his guidance, even when it puts her in a precarious position. Remarkably, when each ruler discovers the truth, he returns Sarai safely to Abram, along with gifts to smooth over the situation.

These incidents not only underscore Sarai's steadfast commitment to Abram but also shed light on a complex truth about their relationship: She was indeed his half-sister, sharing the same father but different mothers (Gen. 20:12). Although this revelation adds a smidgen of truth to their profitable deceptions, it doesn't excuse Abram's decisions which feel strategically necessary but remain ethically contentious. Thankfully, God protects her from being violated, intervening through divine warnings to the rulers.

As time marches on, both Sarai and Abram have a strong desire to build a family. For them, having children is about more than personal fulfillment; it's an essential part of fulfilling their religious and societal obligations. Unfortunately, like many couples today, they struggle with infertility. In their culture, this issue is significant not just personally but also socially. Having no children means the end of the family line and the loss of generational wealth, as any inheritance would then go to someone completely unrelated to them.

You can almost sense Abram's cynicism towards God's delayed promise of an heir in Genesis 15:2, when he says:

> O Lord God, what will you give me, for I continue childless,
> and the heir of my house is Eliezer of Damascus?...You have given
> me no offspring, so a slave born in my house is to be my heir.
> Genesis 15:2

At this time in history, in this culture, when a man has no biological offspring, the inheritance automatically passes to a male slave in the same household.

Slavery is, was, and always will be **ABHORRENT** and **WRONG**.

God hears Abram's concern and assures him that not only will he have an heir but also "no one but **your very own issue** shall be your heir" (Gen. 15:4). In other words, He assures Abram that he himself will be the **biological** father, and the Lord seals this promise with a solemn covenant.

 Please note: There is still no mention of who the mother will be... YET!

Even though Sarai is not mentioned in this conversation between Abram and the Lord, they (rightly) assume the promise includes her. So, they continue diligently working to start a family. For **Y-E-A-R-S**. To no avail.

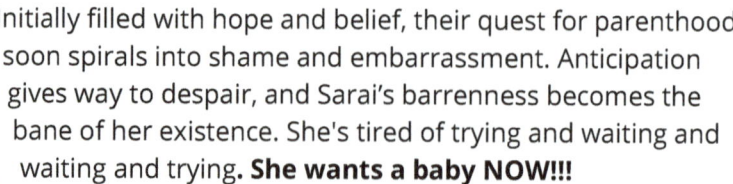

Initially filled with hope and belief, their quest for parenthood soon spirals into shame and embarrassment. Anticipation gives way to despair, and Sarai's barrenness becomes the bane of her existence. She's tired of trying and waiting and waiting and trying. **She wants a baby NOW!!!**

Sarai becomes completely obsessed with manifesting a solution. Since she's not able to conceive, and God promised Abram an heir, she is determined to exhaust all her options which includes using her servant Hagar as a potential surrogate.

Determined to get this show on the road, Sarai insists Abram have sex with Hagar, and it's bittersweet when she conceives right away. Immediately, Hagar's status is elevated in the eyes of everyone—especially her own.

Nine months later, Hagar delivers a baby boy whom they name Ishmael, and Abram falls in love with *his* firstborn son. He dotes on his only child, and grooms him as his heir for the next thirteen years! But then...

Side Note:
We'll work through Hagar's story in the next chapter, but for now, please note that it was perfectly acceptable, even customary, for a barren woman to use her slave as a surrogate. For details about forced surrogacy, see the Spotlight article on page 38.

SOAPBOX MOMENT

When God promises Abram in Genesis 12 that he will be made into a great nation, there is no mention of his wife Sarai.

Many years later, still childless, Abram questions God's promise. It seems like all his possessions will be inherited by a servant born in his home, Eliezer of Damascus. In this patriarchal society, it is customary for a man with no biological heirs to adopt a servant who would "provide for his burial and inherit his estate."¹ To Abram, this is the only conceivable solution.

When God clarifies that Abram's heir will come from his own body, there is still no mention of Sarai. Therefore, when they opt to use a servant as a surrogate—a culturally accepted practice for infertile couples—they are not defying God but acting within the scope of divine revelation available to them at that time.

Each step they take is based on what God has revealed to them. Therefore, we can honor Abram and Sarai's decisions as pragmatic responses to God's plan as it is unveiled over many years. And honestly, isn't that the best any of us can do? So, we take the next right step based on what God has revealed to us in that moment, and trust that "all things work together for good for those who love God, who are called according to his purpose." Romans 8:28

GOD shows up and disrupts Abram's life with a major announcement. Something he's been waiting for. Something that will change *EVERYTHING*!

In Genesis 17, the Lord reveals to Abram that the heir he's been promised is NOT his son Ishmael—it's someone who hasn't even been conceived yet. And, the mother of this child will be Abram's longtime wife: SARAI.

When God at long last reveals the details of His plan to Abram and restates His promise, He does something unprecedented to mark the occasion: **He changes their names.** First, Abram ("exalted father") is changed to Abraham ("father of a multitude"). Then, Sarai ("my princess") is changed to Sarah, which technically means the same thing, but carries a deeper meaning.

> As for Sarai your wife, you shall not call her Sarai,
> but SARAH shall be her name.
> I will bless HER and also give you a son by HER.
> I will bless HER, and
> SHE shall give rise to nations;
> kings of peoples shall come from HER...
> your wife SARAH shall bear you a son,
> and you shall name him Isaac.
> I will establish my covenant with him as an
> everlasting covenant for his offspring after him.
> Genesis 17:15–16 & 19 (emphasis mine)

In the words of Dr. Eli Lizorkin-Eyzenberg, Sarah's name change "signifies that her strength does not belong exclusively to her immediate family, but to the future nation of Israel and even the world-at-large."[2] From now on, instead of living by the names given to them by their families of origin, they are to live by the names given to them by God.

This means each time they speak the other's new name, they proclaim God's promises and a future legacy that will impact the entire world—because when it all comes down, they are in a covenant relationship with God, and He has promised to make their descendants into a "multitude of nations" (Gen 17:4). If you haven't read it yet, please read Genesis 17 for the blow-by-blow.

Take a moment to think about this: How does Abraham react when he hears that SARAH will bear him a son? With praise? Gratitude? Awe?

Well, I hate to break it to you, but Abraham's reaction is a mix of total shock, utter dismay, serious resistance, and awkward laughter.

> Then Abraham fell on his face and laughed and said to himself,
> "Can a child be born to a man who is a hundred years old?
> Can Sarah, who is ninety years old, bear a child?"
> Genesis 17:17

Instead of jumping for joy at the news, Abram lobbies for his teenage son to receive the blessing and inheritance. He *begs* the Lord to allow Ishmael to be the son upon whom His favor rests, but this is not God's plan—**it never was.**

How much of this encounter do you think Abraham shares with Sarah? Hagar? Ishmael? Here's **what we know for sure** about life after God reveals His plan to Abraham:

(1) Abraham and Sarah embrace and start using their new names, *and*

(2) Sarah hasn't bought into the idea of trying to get pregnant again—especially at her age. She remains resigned to Ishmael as their heir.

But then, one day, God. Shows. Up. **LITERALLY.**

Side Note:
Some Christian teachers suggest the visit by three men at Mamre symbolizes a visit from the triune Godhead: Father, Son, and Holy Spirit. Jewish scholars, obviously, disagree, and they are not wrong. While Christians believe in the Holy Trinity, this is not that. When you read this chapter in context, paying close attention to what comes before and what comes after, it's clear two of the visitors are angels, and one is a theophany—God *appearing* as a man, not a fully embodied human like Jesus.

This postcard was painted ca. 1925 and features what many consider to be the Oak of Abraham. This tree fell in 2019, but there are efforts to maintain the stump and a new shoot that has sprung out of it.

One sunny afternoon, three visitors join Abraham in the shade of some trees outside his tent home in Hebron. (*See Side Note on previous page.*)

With hospitality being one of their core values, Abraham and Sarah quickly get to work preparing a refreshing meal for the weary travelers. Abraham prepares to grill out while Sarah heads into the tent to make fresh rolls. While kneading the dough, she eavesdrops on their conversation. She's curious. Who are they? Where are they headed? Why are they here?

It's all rather mundane until one of them delivers a preposterous prediction that Sarah will soon conceive a child. Her reaction is priceless.

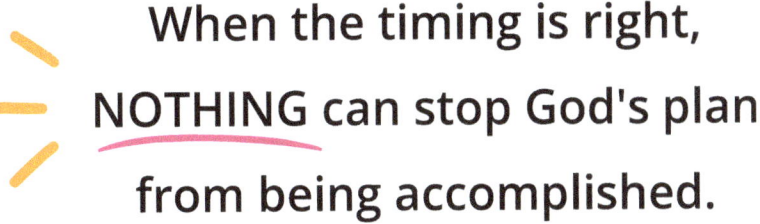

Sarah laughs *to herself* in quiet astonishment. It's **impossible at this age**, isn't it? Her reaction is very similar to Abraham's when God revealed to him that she would mother his child.

When the guests overhear her laughter (maybe she wasn't as quiet as she thought she was?!), they ask her why she laughed. **BUSTED!!!**

With four men staring at her, Sarah becomes afraid and denies that she laughed. Why do you think she is fearful? Why does she laugh at a prediction about the one thing she's been wanting for *literally* decades?

When the timing is right, NOTHING can stop God's plan from being accomplished.

At age 90, not only does she conceive, she carries the baby full-term, *and* survives labor with no epidural. She delivers a bouncing baby boy, navigates all the emotions postpartum, and raises him to follow the ways of the Lord God. They name their baby what God commanded when He revealed Sarah would be his mother—a name that just so happens to reflect their reactions to the prophecy of his birth. They name him Isaac, which means "laughter."

Isn't it a relief to know that Sarah's initial reaction to the prophecy has absolutely *no impact* on its fulfillment?

Sarah's journey through decades of infertility as well as her actions after Isaac is born are far from perfect. Along the way, she makes some significant, mean-spirited mistakes due to low self-esteem and high jealousy. We'll observe some of the more problematic aspects of Sarah's character in the next chapter. For now, suffice it to say, it's a good thing God's faithfulness is based on HIS character, not ours. 🙌

Read more about Sarah's life in **Genesis 11:27-23:20** and **Hebrews 11:8-16**. ✻

Personal Reflections

What stood out to you?

Did reading this chapter prompt further questions?

Look at the cover photo for this chapter and imagine why it was chosen. What do you notice?

Is there someone in your life who reminds you of **Sarah**? Someone who has been loyal to her husband through thick and thin? Or maybe someone who has been wanting a child for a really long time? A woman who has struggled with infertility? For years?

Consider sending her a quick text, an encouraging message, or a longer letter to let her know you're thinking of her today and appreciate the love she shares with the world. Remember, it's not our place to prophesy in God's name without His prompting or direction. Instead, we should focus on listening and holding a nonjudgmental, advice-free space for them. By being empathetic, we provide the deeper, more meaningful support they may need on rough days.

If the woman you thought of is you, please reach out to a trusted friend, mentor, or beloved family member. Ask them to hold space for you to share how today's study has impacted you. For further support, please send a message to the author at: **info@valiantwomenofthebible.com**.

chapter three

Hagar

NAMES GOD

"So she named the Lord who spoke to her,
'You are El-roi,' for she said, 'Have I really seen God
and remained alive after seeing him?'"
Genesis 16:13

Hagar

In the previous chapter, we witnessed Sarai and Abram's brief migration to Egypt during a severe famine in Canaan. While there, the pharaoh took Sarai into his home and, in return, gave Abram "sheep, oxen, male donkeys, male and female slaves, female donkeys, and camels" as a sort-of dowry. However, when he discovered Sarai and Abram were actually married, the pharaoh sent Abram away "with his wife and <u>ALL</u> that he had"—*including the servants.* (*See Gen. 12:10-20*).

Hagar, whose name means "flight" or "foreigner," is Sarai's Egyptian maidservant. In this chapter, as we shift our focus from one woman's hope to another's endurance, we'll see there's a lot more to Hagar than meets the eye. This slave woman has developed a tremendous sense of autonomy, self-worth, and resilience—she is a brave and valiant woman.

To understand Hagar's journey, we need explore the circumstances which bring her into the spotlight. After years of trying to get pregnant with no luck, Sarai takes the next culturally acceptable step: forced surrogacy. (*See page 38 for details about this ancient practice.*) Sarai compels her husband to have sex with her slave: If Hagar conceives, then he will finally have a biological heir.

The practice of offering a female slave (i.e., womb slave) to one's husband **for the purpose of childbearing** is a relatively common practice in the Levant. Dr. Tikva Frymer-Kensky, former Professor of Hebrew Bible and the History of Judaism in the Divinity School at the University of Chicago, explains:

> This practice of surrogacy can be found in a number of ancient Near Eastern texts...In the world of the Ancient Near East, a slave woman could be seen as an incubator, a kind of womb-with-legs.[1]

Our hearts should break for Hagar as she has no rights in this situation—no agency over her body; no right to refuse; no legal claim to her own baby. 💔

22

It's not long until Hagar skips her period. Does she realize that's a sign she might be pregnant? Does she experience morning sickness? Does she crave bread sticks? Or pickle juice?

😳 IT'S JUST EMOTIONS, BABY!

As Hagar's baby bump grows, the truth becomes blatantly obvious, and a noticeable shift occurs in the family dynamics. It starts when Sarai, perhaps for the first time, realizes that *her* infertility is the underlying cause of their childlessness. Until Hagar's condition made it clear, the source of their inability to conceive had remained a painful uncertainty.

At this time, Hagar's emotions are understandably quite different from Sarai's. Aside from being violated by her owners—emotionally by one, physically by the other—Hagar recognizes her status in the family has dramatically tilted in her favor.

Technically, Hagar remains a servant, but everyone knows she is carrying Abram's heir. And although her child will be legally and socially recognized as Sarai's, at this moment in time, **the baby is all hers**. It's *her* body. *Her* baby.

This new and undeniable reality elevates Hagar's sense of self-worth, entitlement, and a level of confidence she likely hasn't experienced until now. Understandably, she begins to despise Sarai, and like her baby bump, it shows.

BABY-MAMA DRAMA 🍼

This pregnancy, so deeply desired and long-awaited, ignites a fierce personality clash reminiscent of the tension and drama we'd expect from a daytime soap opera or reality TV. The air is thick with anticipation and tinged with jealousy and resentment as the relationship triangle of Sarai, Abram, and Hagar devolves in unexpected (and slightly toxic) ways.

Abram is completely loyal and defers to his wife. Combine that with his utter indifference towards Hagar, and Sarai is free to treat her pregnant servant however she wants. The situation deteriorates rapidly.

Sarai is extremely harsh on Hagar, making her life so miserable that she'd rather risk life on her own than stay with the father of her child. So she takes off. She runs away. Pregnant. Alone. Into the desert. What is she thinking?

Hagar eventually finds her way to a natural spring, and there she meets a messenger of the LORD, an angel. He directs her to return home and endure the harsh treatment because only there will she be able to carry the baby full term. The angel promises that her descendants will be greatly increased, and he makes a proclamation about the baby she is carrying:

> And the angel of the Lord said to her, "Now you have conceived and shall bear a son; you shall call him Ishmael, for the Lord has given heed to your affliction. He shall be a wild ass of a man, with his hand against everyone, and everyone's hand against him, and he shall live at odds with all his kin."
> Genesis 16:11–12

This prophecy is COMFORTING to Hagar. Seriously! Given her status as a slave who has been used and mistreated, the idea that her son will possess the qualities of a "wild ass"—independence, strength, and an untamable spirit—brings her solace. It reassures her that Ishmael will be able to fend for himself, resist control, and survive the harsh conditions of his environment, unlike her own constrained existence.

And for the first time (in her life?), Hagar feels authentically seen. Valued. Understood. This is a totally new experience for Hagar, and her response is to do something that NO ONE ELSE in the Bible does: **She names God.** Hagar calls him "*El Roi*" which means "the God who sees me" (Genesis 16:13).

 Just pause for a moment and let this land in your body:
The **ONLY** person in the Bible to give God a name is a **WOMAN**.

This encounter at the spring changes the trajectory of Hagar's life. She returns home, endures maltreatment, carries her baby full-term, delivers a son, and gives him the name Ishmael just as the angel instructed.

🎉 🎉 🎉 And there was much rejoicing!

For the next **thirteen years**, everyone treats Ishmael as Abraham's heir, but when Sarah miraculously conceives and bears a son at the ripe old age of ninety, everything changes. Again.

Sarah immediately falls in love with her baby boy, whom they name Isaac, and no longer has any use for Hagar or her son Ishmael. She perceives each of them as a threat and demands Abraham send them away. *Forever.*

She couldn't care less that Abraham is Ishmael's biological father or that they have raised him as the heir apparent since he was a baby. **Sarah gets what Sarah wants**, and Abraham sends them away. Isn't it intriguing to witness the incredible power Sarah wields over matters of the heart and home?

BACK TO THE DESERT 🐫

Once again, we observe Hagar leaving the safety of her community and heading out into the desert, this time with her teenage son by her side. The two are given minimal provisions, which quickly run out leading to fatigue and dehydration. **Hagar begins to lose hope they will survive this ordeal**.

Hot, weak, and out of options, Hagar has Ishmael lie down under a bush, out of the direct sunlight. Then, unable to bear the sight of her son dying, she distances herself from him and cries out to God from the depth of her soul. Has it all come down to this? What about the prophecy? Where is *El Roi*?

He is indeed there, and this time, the *God who sees* is also the *God who hears*. He **hears** Ishmael, remembers His promise to Hagar, and **opens Hagar's eyes to see** exactly what is needed at that moment: a nearby well of fresh water. 💦 🙌 Mother and son are able to rehydrate, rest, and recuperate. And God remains with them. Over the years, Hagar has the joy of watching her boy grow into a man, a husband, and a father. They remain liberated.

Hagar's story of oppression, sexual exploitation, and deep emotional trauma exposes the dark side of the Abraham and Sarah saga, while at the same time, it spotlights how the God who sees also sustains those who cry out to Him, regardless of their ethnicity, position in society, or economic status.

You can read Hagar's story in <u>Gen. 16-21</u>; she also is alluded to in <u>Gal. 4</u>. 🕊

Laura Zielke

HAGAR IN ISLAMIC TRADITION

Hagar is a key figure in Islamic tradition revered for her faith and amazing perseverance. She is closely associated with the origins of Mecca, and is considered an ancestor of the Prophet Muhammad.

While not named explicitly in the Qur'an, Hagar's story—particularly her time in the wilderness with her son Ishmael—is highlighted in Islamic texts and traditions that demonstrate her deep love for her son.

Tradition holds that after their provisions are gone, and Ishmael cries of thirst, Hagar desperately runs between two hills looking for water. She does this seven times, wearing herself out. At this point, the angel appears stating that God heard Ishmael's cry. The *Women's Islamic Initiative in Spirituality and Equality* (WISE) describes the scene as follows:

> After trying seven times, as she [Hagar] lay despondent,
> Angel Gabriel appeared to her, told her that God had heard
> Ishmael cry and with his wingtip struck the ground open
> to allow a miraculous spring of water to gush forth...
> This well of water [the Zamzam Well] became the bloodline of
> Mecca converting it into a hustling town and eventually leading
> to the development of a new world civilization.[2]

This scene is still re-enacted during Hajj, an annual Islamic pilgrimage to Mecca required of all Muslims who are physically and financially able to perform it. Individuals imitate Hagar's desperation or "striving" by walking briskly from one hill to the other **seven times** "in honor of Hagar's sacrifice." The route between the two hills, Safa and Marwa, is called al-Mas'aa, and it covers a total distance of approximately 2.2 miles.

At the conclusion of the ritual, pilgrims drink fresh water from the Zamzam Well (located between the Kaaba—Islam's holiest site—and the al-Mas'aa) that continues to flow to this very day.[3]

Scan me

⟫ 🎬 SUPPLEMENTAL VIDEO RESOURCE

You can watch a video of pilgrims performing the Saee ritual on YouTube. Click the link below, or scan the QR code with your smart device. **https://bit.ly/vwb-yt-saee**

Above: An inside view of the al-Mas'aa as pilgrims from all over the world perform the Saee
Below: The Kaaba in Mecca, and the directions of the ritual walk [Saee] during Hajj

At each end of this route, the hills of Safa and Marwa are prominently displayed, encased in thick glass to protect them from erosion and the immense crowds that gather here each year.

Over the centuries, the path itself has evolved significantly. Originally a simple dirt path, the al-Mas'aa is now a tiled walkway housed within a vast, air-conditioned structure.

Equipped with traffic control systems and accessibility features, including a special lane for pilgrims with wheelchairs or electric carts, the al-Mas'aa is setup so everyone is able to participate in the ritual.

Personal Reflections

What stood out to you?

Did reading this chapter prompt further questions?

Look at the cover photo for this chapter and imagine why it was chosen. What do you notice?

Is there someone in your life who reminds you of **Hagar**? Someone who overcame traumatic life experiences and created a life for herself due to pure grit and a strong faith in God's provision?

Consider sending her a quick text, encouraging message, or longer letter to let her know you're thinking of her today. Acknowledge her strength and/or share one way she inspires you to rely on God.

If the woman you thought of is you, please reach out to a trusted friend, mentor, or beloved family member. Ask them to hold space for you to share how today's study has impacted you. For further support, please send a message to the author at <u>info@valiantwomenofthebible.com</u>.

View from Mount Sinai at sunrise. Beautiful mountain landscape in Egypt

chapter four

Rachel & Leah

SISTER WIVES

"Now Laban had two daughters, the name of the elder
was Leah, and the name of the younger was Rachel.
Leah's eyes were weak, but Rachel was graceful and beautiful."
Genesis 29:16–17

Rachel & Leah

When we first meet Rachel, she's working for the family business: Her father, Laban, owns a lot of sheep, and she is a shepherd. 🐑 Rachel cares for her dad's flock ensuring the sheep are safe and have everything they need for a long, healthy life—especially access to clean, uncontaminated water.

Since there is no creek or river nearby, she and other local shepherds rely on fresh water from a well—one they protect by covering it with a massive stone.

One ordinary day, Rachel guides her flock to the well. It's a familiar scene: all the regulars are chit-chatting near the original water cooler while their flocks lay in a nearby field. As she approaches the well, she recognizes everyone with one exception: There's a stranger in their midst.

Seeing her, the stranger springs into action and single-handedly removes the stone. Not only that, he also waters Rachel's flock providing her a much-appreciated break. 💪

Following all this gallantry, Jacob greets her with a platonic kiss and introduces himself as her cousin, revealing his mother Rebekah and her father Laban are siblings. (*See Side Note.*)

Side Note:
Sarah and Abraham's son, Isaac, marries a woman named **Rebekah**. I'm not covering Rebekah's story in this book, so please allow me to remind you of something that is quite relevant here: Rebekah is famous for encouraging Jacob, her favorite son, to deceive his father, Isaac, in order to receive the family blessing basically stealing it from his twin brother Esau. This is important because we're about to learn that Rebekah wasn't the only deceiver in her family.

Leaving her sheep at the well, Rachel runs to share the news of her cousin's arrival with her father. Though we don't know exactly what she tells him, it's safe to assume she mentions Jacob's removing the stone cover from the well and watering her sheep, because Laban drops everything and rushes back to greet his nephew and welcomes him with open arms. (♫ *Cue the dark, ominous, sinister music, because Laban is a schemer who is always crafting plans for his own material gain.*)

Uncle Laban invites Jacob into his home and puts him right to work. After a month, he offers to compensate Jacob for his service and inquires, "What shall your wages be?" (Genesis 29:15).

SOMETHING TO THINK ABOUT...

*As Laban poses this question to Jacob, I can't help but wonder if he gestures towards his daughters. It's at this moment we learn that he has not one, but **two** unmarried daughters. Could he be offering them as compensation? Leah, his eldest daughter, is described as having "soft eyes," while Rachel, her younger sister, is noted for being "graceful and beautiful." Based on what we know from the passage, it appears Laban has no other children.*

When Laban asks, "What shall your wages be?" Jacob follows his heart, and asks for Rachel to be his wife. His uncle agrees on one condition: Jacob will have to prove himself by working for him for seven years before they wed.

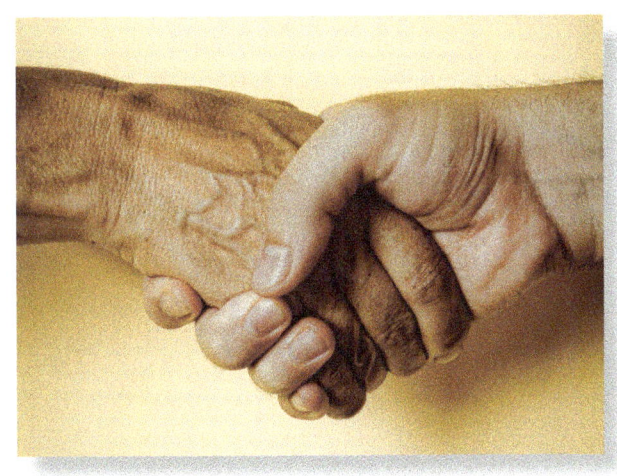

♫ *Cue the sinister music again, because Laban's plan is working. Mwahahaha!*

⏩ **FAST FORWARD 7 YEARS** to the time when Jacob and Rachel are **FINALLY GETTING MARRIED**. The father of the bride throws a big party for everyone in the neighborhood, and then they are married... *OR ARE THEY?*

PLOT TWIST!

In an unexpected (at least to Jacob) plot twist, Laban sends his **eldest** daughter **Leah**—NOT RACHEL 😳—into the honeymoon suite to make their union official, which she does. And though it seems unthinkable that a man would not recognize his fiancée after seven years, we must be careful not to project our modern expectations of romantic relationships on the ancient world.

Edith Deen, in her seminal book *All the Women of the Bible*, notes it was customary for a bride to wear a veil during the wedding. After the ceremony, she would be conducted "to the bedchamber of her husband in silence and darkness,"[1] and the groom would not see her face until after the marriage is consummated. *(See "Digging Deeper" on the next page for other theories.)*

This whole marriage debacle was an inversion of an earlier trick Jacob played on his twin brother Esau:

Rebekah (Laban's sister) encouraged Jacob to pretend to be his **older** brother, Esau, thereby **tricking** her husband into giving his blessing to the **wrong** (younger) son.	Laban (Rebekah's brother) encouraged Leah to pretend to be her **younger** sister, Rachel, thereby **tricking** his nephew into consummating a marriage with the **wrong** (older) daughter.

🤔 Do you think Jacob ever realized this "law of the harvest"? You reap what you sow (Galatians 6:7).

THE CONFRONTATION

When Jacob confronts his uncle about this treachery, Laban explains their custom of marrying off the oldest daughter first (better late than never), and offers Rachel to Jacob (again), but on two conditions:

1. He must complete the wedding week of festivities with Leah, AND
2. He must agree to continue working for Laban for seven more years.

Jacob agrees, and a week later, marries Rachel. Now, he has two wives, and each comes with her own maidservant or "womb slave." *(See page 38.)*

DIGGING DEEPER

Jewish rabbis and scholars, as well as their Christian counterparts, have debated Jacob's first marriage for well over a thousand years.

In his article on *TheTorah.com*, "How Is It Possible that Jacob Mistakes Leah for Rachel?" Rabbi Dr. Zev Farber explores a few different theories about Laban's ruse.

One popular theory is that Laban threw the party for a single purpose: to get Jacob so drunk he wouldn't know which daughter he was with, and his deception would go off without a hitch.

Another theory is that this ancient culture exercised "extreme modesty" where the newly united couple would copulate in darkness and silence.

Rabbi Dr. Farber offers another, more plausible interpretation:

"After Jacob makes the deal with Laban and goes off to watch Laban's sheep for seven years, Laban either tells his older daughter Leah that she is to marry Jacob, or says nothing at all. Either way, when Leah is brought to Jacob that night, she believes that he wanted to marry her. Rachel likely believed the same thing."[2]

Of course, that doesn't address Jacob's legit surprise in the morning.

ONE MAN WITH FOUR WOMEN: WHAT COULD *POSSIBLY* GO WRONG? 😂

Rachel and Leah are the only "sister wives" recorded in the Bible. Even though they share the same husband and do what married couples do, they do not share Jacob's heart. Nor do they share the same level of fertility.

LEAH IS FERTILE, BUT UNLOVED. RACHEL IS LOVED, BUT BARREN.

Although Jacob loves Rachel, he regularly sleeps with both of them. When Leah becomes pregnant, the baby-mama drama takes the tension to a whole new level. By the time Leah delivers her fourth son, being the apple of Jacob's eye is no longer enough for Rachel. She is jealous of her sister's ability to produce babies, and decides to take matters into her own hands—just like Jacob's grandmother Sarah did back in the day.

Rachel compels Jacob to have sex with her handmaid (i.e., womb slave), Bilhah, according to custom. If Bilhah conceives, the baby will be considered hers. Rachel's plan works: Bilhah gets pregnant and delivers a baby boy.

At this, Leah decides to up the ante: She spurs Jacob to have sex with her handmaid, Zilpah, hoping for the same result. She gets it. Zilpah conceives.

In time, the **three** women give birth to **TEN SONS:**

Leah's sons:
Reuben, Simeon, Levi, Issachar, Judah, & Zebulun

Zilpah's sons:
Gad & Asher

Bilhah's sons:
Dan & Naphtali

Can you imagine a household full of 10 boys?! God bless those mamas! We know that the boys had at least one sister, DINAH. Unfortunately, since female births were less commonly recorded, there is no record of any other daughters. This is reflective of the cultural norms of the ancient Near East. **Dinah is the daughter of Jacob and Leah.**

BUT WAIT, THERE'S MORE!

After Jacob has fathered ten sons—**NONE** of them by his favorite wife Rachel—God surprises everyone with a new and unexpected pregnancy. Much to the delight of *almost* everyone—Rachel finally conceives and bears a son whom they name Joseph. *(This is the same Joseph who is later gifted an "amazing technicolor dreamcoat" by his proud papa and later sold into slavery by his older brothers.)*

⏩ **FAST-FORWARD A FEW MORE YEARS:** Jacob is ready to return to his homeland, along with his two wives, two womb-slaves, eleven sons, and at least one daughter. When Jacob, Rachel, and Leah discuss moving away from Laban's homestead, we finally hear from the women themselves.

The sisters hold nothing back as they express their raw, authentic feelings about their father. Speaking as one, they reveal his true character:

> Is there any portion or inheritance left to us in our father's house? Are we not regarded by him as foreigners? For HE HAS SOLD US, and he has been using up the money given for us.
> Genesis 31:14–16 (emphasis mine)

In her comments on Genesis in the *Women's Bible Commentary*, Susan Niditch highlights how remarkable it is to hear women from that time speak so critically about their treatment and status:

> Nowhere else in Hebrew scriptures is a proper marriage described as a father's selling (*makar*) his daughters... Thus, bitterly and poignantly, the daughters of Laban describe themselves in their relationship to their father as exploited and dispossessed slaves, treated as foreign women unrelated to him...They state that their rights have not been upheld. Indirectly, they call attention to a world in which people are bought and sold.[3]

It's around this time that Rachel becomes pregnant again—and the timing is less than ideal. She goes into labor while they are on the move to Canaan, experiencing severe complications. Rachel delivers her second son and lives long enough to name him Ben-oni ("son of my sorrow"). Then, she dies. 😞

Jacob is devastated by this loss, but he's not about to call his baby "son of my sorrow." He immediately changes his son's name to Benjamin ("son of the right hand"). Was this a way to honor the memory of his right-hand woman?

Laura Zielke

JACOB'S FAMILY TREE

Joseph and Benjamin are the youngest of Jacob's children, but they are easily his favorite sons since their mother was his one true love.

Jacob fathered twelve sons with Leah, Rachel, and their womb slaves, Bilhah and Zilpah. These sons became the founders of the Twelve Tribes of Israel.

Note: Instead of a single tribe bearing Joseph's name, his legacy is continued through his two sons, Ephraim and Manasseh, with each of them comprising a half-tribe.

You can read more about Rachel and Leah in Genesis 29-35.

Look for the time Leah bartered a night with Jacob for some of her son's mandrakes and the time Rachel stole her father's "family gods." ✺

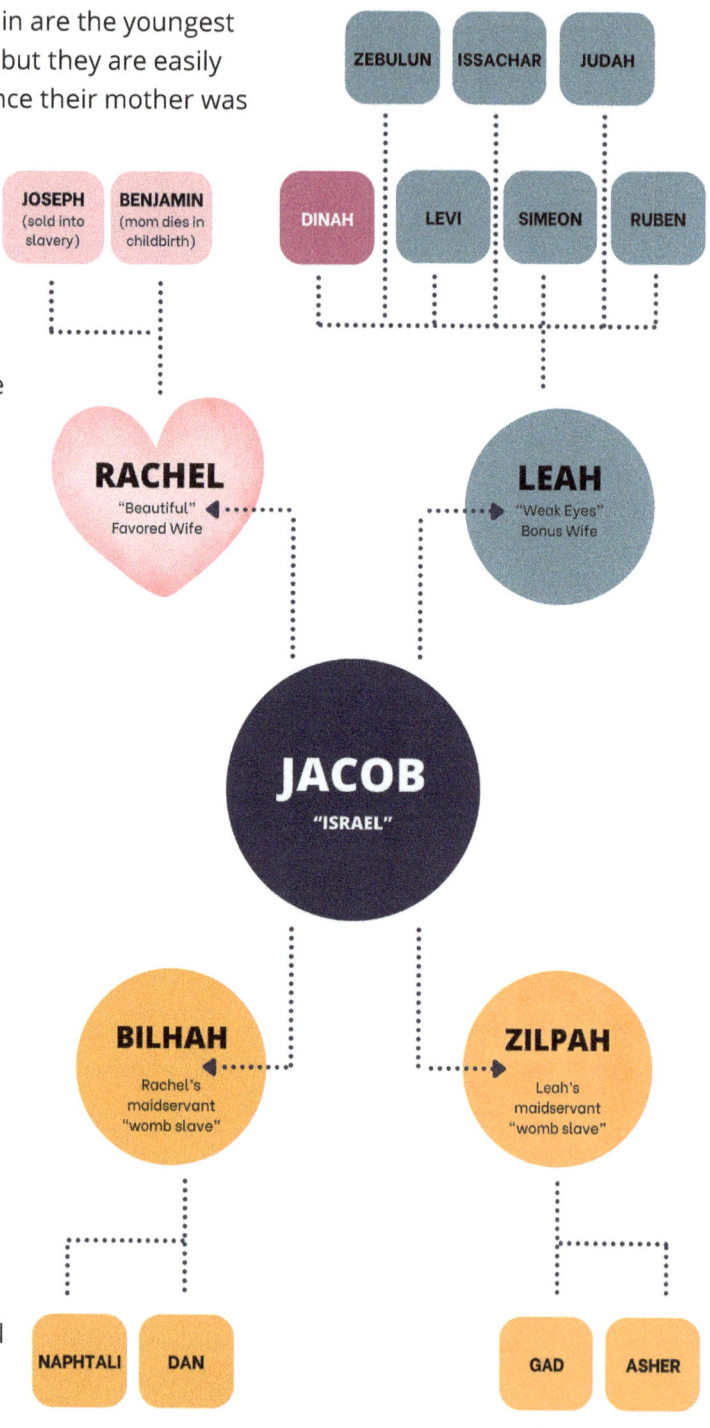

ZEBULUN ISSACHAR JUDAH

JOSEPH (sold into slavery) BENJAMIN (mom dies in childbirth)

DINAH LEVI SIMEON RUBEN

RACHEL
"Beautiful" Favored Wife

LEAH
"Weak Eyes" Bonus Wife

JACOB
"ISRAEL"

BILHAH
Rachel's maidservant "womb slave"

ZILPAH
Leah's maidservant "womb slave"

NAPHTALI DAN

GAD ASHER

Personal Reflections

What stood out to you?

Did reading this chapter prompt further questions?

Look at the cover photo for this chapter and imagine why it was chosen. What do you notice?

Is there someone in your life who reminds you of **Leah**? Someone who has a physical challenge or suffers from an invisible chronic illness? Someone who is consistently underestimated or dismissed? A woman who refuses to let society dictate her happiness?

Consider sending her a quick text, encouraging message, or longer letter to let her know you're thinking of her today. Acknowledge her resilience and/or share one way she inspires you to rely on God.

Is there someone who reminds you of **Rachel**? Someone who is beautiful inside and out? Someone who loves her husband, wants children, but has struggled with infertility for a really long time?

Consider sending her a quick text, encouraging message, or longer letter to let her know you're thinking of her today. Acknowledge her beautiful character and/or share one way she inspires you to rely on God.

If either of the women you thought of is you, please reach out to a trusted friend, mentor, or beloved family member. Ask them to hold space for you to share how today's study has impacted you. For further support, please send a message to the author at <u>info@valiantwomenofthebible.com</u>.

THE WOMB-SLAVE
UNDERSTANDING FORCED SURROGACY IN THE HEBREW BIBLE

In the ancient Near East, fertility and procreation were crucial for maintaining family lineage, social status, economic support, and fulfilling religious imperatives. Women who found themselves unable to conceive experienced deep emotional distress and social isolation. In an effort to ease the pain and fulfill their obligation to their husbands, a new practice emerged: the barren wife would offer her servant, or acquire one, as a means to ensure the continuity of the family line through her borrowed womb.

Scholars have provided insightful perspectives on this ancient norm. Dr. Wilda C. Gafney, in her work *Womanist Midrash*, coined the term "womb slave" to describe these involuntary surrogates.[1] Similarly, Dr. Tikvah Frymer-Kensky likened such a slave to "an incubator, a kind of 'womb-with-legs.'"[2]

This practice of using handmaids as womb slaves eventually became woven into the fabric of familial and societal expectations and spread across the ancient Near East. Archaeologists have discovered numerous cuneiform texts that reference this centuries-long practice, including Old Assyrian tablets from Anatolia (ca. 20th to 18th centuries BCE), the Code of Hammurabi from the Old Babylonian Empire (ca. 1792-1750 BCE), the Nuzi tablets from the Mitanni Empire (ca. 15th-14th century BCE).

It's through this cultural lens we understand Sarai's decision to use her servant Hagar as a surrogate, resulting in the birth of a son for Abram, and Rachel's use of Bilhah, resulting in two sons for Jacob.

 But then, there's a shift.

Leah uses Zilpah as a womb slave—but not due to her infertility. Leah has already birthed four sons! Strategically, Leah uses Zilpah to compete with Rachel (via Bilhah) and maintain her status in the family. Zilpah's story is the perfect example of how easily "rationalized exploitation" can mutate and spread.

The womb-slave stories provide insight into Israel's complex prehistory and serve as an object lesson about how easily societal norms can be manipulated to take advantage of the vulnerable and marginalized.

These stories force us to confront this uncomfortable truth: Any society can distort its most foundational values and normalize oppression. It's a pattern, and it's easy to spot early on. Oppressors often start by justifying exploitation in "limited cases."

Those in power claim they need to subjugate others "only in certain situations"; however, as domination spreads, excuses multiply until all the original constraints disappear. Eventually, the force of sheer power obliterates any need for justification.

Bit by bit, yesterday's rare exceptions transform into today's typical practice, and oppression by the strong persists because it can.

Therefore, it's our responsibility as people of faith to do more than merely witness the world's injustices. We are called to imagine what a world rooted in justice and love might look like—and then work to make that vision a reality.

He has told you, O mortal, what is good, and what does the Lord require of you but to do justice and to love kindness and to walk humbly with your God? Micah 6:8

In order to fulfill this commission, we must be close enough to diverse humans to understand and empathize with their experiences. Jesus modeled this. Proximity is the key to transforming our intentions into actions that honor every individual's inherent dignity.

To forge a just and equitable society, we must question and dismantle oppressive systems and rigorously confront our own biases. We do this by recognizing and valuing the image of God that exists within *every* human (Genesis 1:27). When we practice this, we reduce the marginalization and oppression of people based on their marital status, ability to have children, physical or intellectual abilities, ethnicity, education, religion, gender, sexual orientation, etc.

We are ___ALL___ image bearers.

chapter five

Shiphrah & Puah

REBEL MIDWIVES

"But the midwives feared God; they did not do as the
king of Egypt commanded them...They let the boys live."
Exodus 1:17

Shiphrah & Puah

When we first meet Shiphrah and Puah, they are in the court of a pharaoh in Egypt. They are midwives in his kingdom and about to receive very specific instructions from the "god" himself.

The setting of their story is roughly a few hundred years after the death of Rachel's firstborn son, Joseph, who had risen to be second in command in Egypt during a famine that affected the whole Near East.*

Suffice it to say, at this point in history, the descendants of Jacob (now called "Hebrews") had been living in Egypt long enough to flourish as a people group— they were fruitful and multiplied!

Water Channel in Egypt with a Pyramid in the Background

When this particular pharaoh realizes the foreigners not only outnumber the Egyptians but are also "more mighty," he acts preemptively to take them down a notch by pressing them into forced labor.

Much to his surprise, they build his cities *and* make lots of mighty Hebrew babies. 💪

* Since our focus for this book is on women, not men, I won't be covering the history of when Jacob's family migrated to Egypt as famine refugees. You can read the full narrative in Genesis 37-50. This story takes place around 400 years later.

PHARAOH'S "PLAN B"

In an effort to stunt their population growth without completely diminishing his workforce, the pharaoh commissions Shiphrah and Puah with a special assignment. (*Please read the **Mega Side Note** on the next page for important information about the ethnic background of these "midwives to the Hebrews."*)

Normally, their job is to help expectant mothers deliver healthy babies; however, this time, the paranoid and powerful pharaoh flips their job description on its head.

Their new mission, should they choose to accept it (do they have a choice?) is to MURDER every Hebrew baby boy at the moment of his birth.

Can you imagine how they felt when they received this command? The ethical and moral dilemmas are enough to bring on a serious migraine.

Side Note:
There's something else you should know about these remarkable women: *Each of them is barren.* Both Shiphrah and Puah help other women do something they themselves have never done: birth a baby. They could be resentful and bitter and comply with Pharaoh's order. But they aren't, and they don't.

The midwives, however, feared God and did <u>not</u> do what the king of Egypt had told them to do; THEY LET THE BOYS LIVE! Exodus 1:17 (emphasis mine)

These midwives are rebels. **By defying the pharaoh's orders, they are risking their own lives.** But they would rather die than murder newborn babies.

It is not long until the pharaoh discovers their disobedience. He is irate and insists Shiphrah and Puah appear before him to explain this flagrant affront to his authority. What will they say to this Egyptian "god"?

MIDWIVES: HEBREW OR EGYPTIAN?

There's an ongoing debate about whether or not Shiphrah and Puah were "Hebrew midwives" or "midwives to the Hebrews." This might seem like semantics, but the question is actually about their ethnicity. **Were the women of Hebrew or Egyptian descent?**

Traditional commentaries identify the women as Hebrews; however, the storyline implies they were Egyptian. The text is ambiguous, so we have to look at the context and sources outside the Bible (a.k.a. "extrabiblical" evidence) for clues.

✅ Clue #1: Multi-Cultural Familiarity
They were familiar with both Hebrew and Egyptian birth customs.

✅ Clue #2: Common Sense
It is unlikely the pharaoh would entrust the murder of Hebrew babies to Hebrew midwives.

✅ Clue #3: Manuscript Evidence
The Septuagint was created in the 3rd century B.C.
The first Greek translation of the Hebrew Bible, *The Septuagint,* identifies them as "midwives of the Hebrews" (Exodus 1:16).

✅ Clue #4: Extra-biblical Evidence
Dates to 2nd century A.D.
Josephus, a famous Jewish historian from the first century, describes the women as "the Egyptian midwives" in *Antiquities,* 2:206-207.[1]

✅ Clue #5: Cairo Geniza Fragment
Some fragments date back to the 9th century A.D.
An ancient fragment of text that lists Shiphrah and Puah as "righteous Gentiles" alongside other non-Jewish women mentioned in the Torah. As Rabbi Ana Bonnheim explains:

There is an incredible fragment of a text from the Cairo Geniza... that recognizes Shiphrah and Puah as Egyptians. It's a list of biblical righteous gentiles, and it includes the midwives. The context of the fragment has been lost, but the list remains — and Shiphrah and Puah are on it, along with women like Hagar and Zipporah.[2]

Based on these fantastic clues and basic common sense, I am comfortable asserting:

Shiphrah and Puah were EGYPTIAN midwives to the Hebrews.

Stories like this remind us that God's work is bigger and more inclusive than we imagine.

Valiant Women of the Bible, Volume One

The response of the midwives is creatively cunning. Implying it's not their fault, they tell the pharaoh:

The Hebrew women are
not like the Egyptian women,
they are vigorous and give birth
before the midwives arrive
Exodus 1:19

...And, besides that, the chariot traffic in that part of town is ridiculous!

These rebellious midwives are a *major* blessing to the Hebrew people.

Had it not been for their unwavering determination to disobey the pharaoh's orders, the future of the Hebrews would have been drastically different.

THE BARREN BLESSED WITH BABIES

Because of their bravery in the face of opposition and their commitment to saving the lives of Hebrew baby boys, God bestows a special blessing on both Shiphrah and Puah. Each woman gives birth to children of her own!

You can read Shiphrah and Puah's story in **Exodus 1**. 🕊

Personal Reflections

What stood out to you?

Did reading this chapter prompt further questions?

Look at the cover photo for this chapter and imagine why it was chosen. What do you notice?

Is there someone in your life who reminds you of **Shiphrah** and **Puah**? Someone who refused to do the wrong thing even though her superior(s) insisted on it? Someone who took a stand for the right thing even though it ended up costing her dearly?

Consider sending her a quick text, uplifting message, or longer letter to let her know you're thinking of her today. Acknowledge her courage and commitment to justice, and/or share one way she inspires you to rely on God for everything.

If the woman you thought of is you, please send a message to the author at **info@valiantwomenofthebible.com** so we can encourage you!

View of the Ancient Temples in Luxor, Egypt

chapter six

Jochebed & Miriam

BRAVE SLAVES

"The name of Amram's wife was Jochebed, daughter of Levi,
who was born to Levi in Egypt, and she bore to Amram:
Aaron, Moses, and their sister Miriam."
Numbers 26:59

Jochebed & Miriam

When we first meet Jochebed, we don't learn her name. She is simply referred to as a woman from the tribe of Levi, married to a man from the same tribe. They are unnamed, as are all the main characters in Exodus 2:1-9.

We learn the unnamed couple is living in bondage in Egypt, and like many Hebrews in their situation, they are fruitful and multiply.

Levi was one of the 12 sons of Jacob. His mom was Leah, and his descendants became the Levites, the priestly tribe of Israel

She is married to Amram, and they already have two children: Miriam and Aaron. The story, recorded in the second chapter of *Exodus*, concerns the birth of their third child, Moses.

The events in this narrative occur after the pharaoh realizes Shiphrah and Puah are disobeying his orders. He's so angered by their actions (or inactions) that he orders *any* and *every* Egyptian to toss Hebrew baby boys into the Nile.

Side Note:
Carol Meyers observes that Jochebed is mentioned by name only in two places in the Bible: Exodus 6:20 and Numbers 26:59. Both of these references appear in genealogical listings, underscoring her importance in the lineage of Israel's leaders."[1]

It's around this time that Jochebed delivers her third child, a beautiful baby boy, and hides him from the Egyptians. Is it possible that the Egyptian midwives, Shiphrah and Puah, help deliver the baby who will grow up to deliver all Hebrews out of bondage in Egypt? Possibly. We can't know for certain.

What we do know is that the family figures out a way to hide the baby for three months. This is astounding when you consider (1) Jochebed no longer has her baby bump, (2) newborns are not the quietest creatures on earth, and (3) the other two young children had to keep the family secret.

But. Somehow. They. Do. It. 🙌

Photo (Opposite): Nile River Valley

THREE MONTHS LATER...

After three months, the family can no longer hide their beautiful baby, and they must decide what to do with him. Instead of risking his certain death at the hands of random Egyptians, Jochebed comes up with a plan to save his life. She takes one of her papyrus baskets and seals it with pitch to make it watertight. Once it's ready, she places her son in it, and she and Miriam head down to the river to a place frequented by the pharaoh's daughter and her attendants. They carefully place the basket in the reeds near the shore, and Miriam keeps watch from a distance.

> **> Jochebed's faith God will send someone to rescue him is breathtaking. <**

We have no idea how much time elapses between the baby's placement in the water and his being found, but we do know her plan works! 🙌

Noticing the basket in the water (a gift from the gods?), the princess sends a servant to retrieve it. Inside, she discovers a **Hebrew** baby boy. His cries melt her heart. Overcome with compassion, the pharaoh's daughter decides to keep him for herself.

Side Note:
Exodus 7:7 describes Aaron as three years older than Moses. Because of his age, his life was not in jeopardy due to the pharaoh's evil command to kill all the Hebrew baby boys. Miriam is the eldest of the three children—old enough to follow the basket and speak with the pharaoh's daughter. Some Jewish scholars hold that Miriam was sixteen years old when Moses was born, but there is no consensus. Others record her as young as five years old when Moses is born.

It's around this time that Miriam "happens" upon the group of women gathered at the shore. Noticing the princess holding a crying baby, she bravely approaches and respectfully offers to find a Hebrew woman to nurse it. The princess is amiable, so Miriam heads straight home and returns with Jochebed, never revealing that she is the baby's mother. The princess offers to compensate her for nursing the baby until he is weaned. *What a day!* 😜

THE BIRTH LEGEND OF SARGON

There is a notable parallel between the birth story of Moses and the ancient Near Eastern 'Birth Legend of Sargon,' who founded the Akkadian Empire.

In this legend, Sargon's mother places him in a reed basket sealed with pitch and sets him adrift in the Euphrates River, where he is eventually rescued and raised by a new family.

Since Sargon lived over 1,000 years before Moses, some scholars suggest that the biblical account of Moses' birth and rescue from the Nile River might be a derivative of Sargon's story. However, others (like me) caution against this interpretation, pointing out that just because the stories are similar doesn't necessarily mean one is copied from the other, as **correlation does not imply causation.**

Additionally, the oldest fragments of the Sargon Birth Legend only date back to 700 BCE, which is actually hundreds of years after Moses' birth, according to traditional biblical chronology. This raises the possibility that the Sargon legend could have been influenced by oral traditions passed down through generations in Jewish families.

2015-12 Birth Sargon of Akkad Louvre-AO 7673

Bonus Trivia: *The Birth Legend of Sargon* was discovered in the Royal Library of Ashurbanipal in **Nineveh**, the ancient capital of Assyria, where Jonah was sent to prophesy. Is it possible he shared about Moses while he was there?

This scene is part of an overarching theme in *Exodus*, where the pharaoh is repeatedly shown to be powerless compared to the God of the Hebrews. Even his own daughter adds to his disgrace by intentionally defying his orders and raising the child, whom she names Moses (meaning something like "pulled from the water") in the palace right under his nose.

⏩ FAST FORWARD 40+ YEARS

At the age of 80 (Exodus 7:7), Moses is called by the Lord to deliver the Hebrew people out of slavery in Egypt. This familiar account from *Exodus* describes how Moses guides them to *and through* the Red Sea.

After crossing over, and with the Egyptians no longer in pursuit, the people pause to express gratitude to God for their miraculous escape. It's time to celebrate their newfound freedom and independence.

By this time, Miriam is either in or near her nineties, but age is just a number, right?! Joining the celebration, she quickly locates her tambourine and leads a procession of dancing, tambourine-toting women in song:

> Sing to the Lord, for he has triumphed gloriously;
> the horse and his rider he has thrown into the sea.
> Exodus 15:20–21

In this instance, Miriam's actions echo those of her brother Moses, which is nice. However, she doesn't always follow his lead. As a respected prophet herself, there are times when she thinks Moses is off his rocker and believes (knows?) she could do a better job—*probably because she's the oldest.* 😂

MIRIAM'S DESTRUCTIVE AMBITION

During their 40-year wilderness journey, Miriam and Aaron grow increasingly frustrated with Moses' leadership, especially after his second marriage to a Cushite (Black African[2]) woman. The elderly siblings grumble amongst themselves, complaining that Moses is not the *only* one in the family who hears from God. They do, too!

Miriam, confident in her leadership abilities and self-righteous in her judgments, decides it's time to take a stand and do something. As a recognized prophet in her own right, she feels ready to take charge; however, there is one thing she hasn't considered:

> **By taking a stand against God's chosen leader,
> she is taking a stand against God.**

And this rebellious attitude, especially since it's being acted out by someone as prominent as Miriam, is not allowed to stand. In an incredible moment, God meets the siblings at the Tabernacle and confronts their insubordination resulting in Miriam's being struck with serious skin condition: leprosy. 🤢

THE MERNEPTAH STELE

A stele (STEEL-ee) is an ancient upright stone slab bearing inscriptions, carvings, or reliefs. Stelae were used as tombstones, boundary markers, and commemorations of military victories. The Merneptah Stele (ca. 1205 BCE) is significant because it features the earliest mention of "Israel" outside the Bible. This Egyptian monument lists Israel not as a nation but as a people[3], hinting at their distinct societal role during the Late Bronze Age. This stele confirms Israel's existence at that time and helps integrate biblical narratives with the historical and geopolitical landscape at that time. It sheds light on the life of the early Israelite people and their interactions with surrounding powers like Egypt.

Merneptah Stele, ca. 1205 BCE

Standing with her, Miriam's brothers immediately cry out to the Lord to spare her life, and He relents, allowing the condition to heal within a week. While she is afflicted, she is cast out of the camp; however, the people don't move again until she is restored in the community—she is that important.

You can learn more about Jochebed, Miriam, and the pharaoh's daughter in the following passages: <u>Exodus 2-15</u> and <u>Numbers 12</u>. ✺

Personal Reflections

What stood out to you?

Did reading this chapter prompt further questions?

Look at the cover photo for this chapter and imagine why it was chosen. What do you notice?

Is there someone in your life who reminds you of **Jochebed**? Someone who took a stand for her child(ren) even though it put her in danger to do it? Someone whose faith gave her the courage to take a big risk that paid off because God was with her?

Consider sending her a quick text, encouraging message, or longer letter to let her know you're thinking of her today. Acknowledge her courage in the face of the unknown and how she encourages your walk with God.

Is there someone in your life who reminds you of **Miriam**? Someone who always strives to do the right thing? Someone who is a natural leader? Someone whose ambition can sometimes be a liability, but who always returns to a place of humble confidence?

Consider sending her a quick text, encouraging message, or longer letter to let her know you're thinking of her today. Acknowledge her strengths and how she inspires your walk with God.

If the woman you thought of is you, please send a message to the author at: <u>info@valiantwomenofthebible.com</u> so we can bear witness to your story.

HISTORICAL OVERVIEW
Key Developments from the Exodus to the Monarchy

This narrative timeline highlights the major phases in the earliest history of Israel as described in the Hebrew Bible, from their deliverance out of slavery in Egypt to the conquest of the Holy Land to the establishment of a kingdom. Up until their first king was anointed, the Israelites were governed as a theocracy.

 A "theocracy" is a unique form of governance where GOD is acknowledged as the supreme authority.

In ancient Israel (pre-monarchy), the theocracy was managed by priests, judges, and prophets, considered representatives of God on Earth. These leaders guided the Israelites based on their interpretations of divine commandments and laws, shaped by their understanding and the prevailing worldview.

THE EXODUS FROM EGYPT
Moses led the Israelites out of Egypt through the Red Sea. After their miraculous crossing, the Israelites endured numerous trials and repeatedly experienced divine provision on their way to Mt. Sinai, where Moses received the Ten Commandments—twice. 😉 This journey not only shaped their identity but also solidified their trust in God as their leader and provider, thereby establishing their theocracy.

40 YEARS IN THE WILDERNESS
Following their stay at Mt. Sinai, the Hebrews lived as nomads for 40 years—a crucial period of spiritual development and religious observance, marked by regular animal sacrifices at a portable Tabernacle. This experience is recorded in *Exodus* and *Numbers*. Prior to his death, Moses* provided detailed guidance for covenant life. In a mix of reflection and forward-looking advice, he stressed obedience to God for blessings and dire consequences for disobedience. Comprising the books of *Deuteronomy* (for covenant life) and *Leviticus* (for the priests, as well as the wider community), these guidelines equipped them to maintain their covenant relationship with God.

THE CONQUEST OF CANAAN
Moses' successor, Joshua, led the Israelites into Canaan, also known as the "Holy Land." The conquest involved roughly seven years of military campaigns, after which the conquered land was divided among the Twelve Tribes of Israel. The book of *Joshua* details these battles as well as the process of settling and establishing control over the land.

THE PERIOD OF THE JUDGES
Following Joshua's death, the Israelites were ruled by a series of "judges"—charismatic leaders like Deborah, Gideon, Jephthah, and Samson—who governed and fought to deliver them from the oppression of neighboring peoples. Recorded in the book of *Judges*, this period was characterized by a recurring cycle: the Israelites would turn away from God, face oppression, repent and cry out for help, and then experience divine deliverance.

THE TRANSITION TO A MONARCH
Eventually, seeking stability and to be more like the neighboring nations, the Israelites demanded a king. Hannah's son, Samuel, a prophet and the last judge, heeded this call and anointed Saul as the first king of Israel in the town of Gibeah. The establishment of the monarchy is detailed in the Books of *Samuel*.

This shift from theocracy to monarchy marked a fundamental change in Israel, impacting both governance and spirituality. It introduced new challenges in maintaining a divine covenant within a political monarchy and set the stage for complex interactions between faith and power that would shape their future as a nation.

---

* *There is considerable debate about when The Torah (a.k.a. the first five books of the Bible) was written. While some Bible teachers insist Moses wrote every word of it (except the account of his own death), there is a growing consensus among biblical scholars that The Torah was compiled by multiple authors during the Babylonian Exile hundreds of years later.*

chapter seven

Rahab

HARLOT HERO

"By faith Rahab the prostitute did not perish
with those who were disobedient, because
she had received the spies in peace."
Hebrews 11:31

Rahab

We first meet Rahab at her home located between the walls of Jericho, the City of Palms. 🌴🌴🌴 *(See Side Note below.)* As an unmarried Canaanite sex worker, Rahab is **triply marginalized** in the biblical narrative. Despite the odds being stacked against her, she becomes a hero to the Israelites—especially the spy who loved her. 😉

Side Note:
Ancient Jericho (pre-wall-drop) was surrounded by two walls with around 12-15 feet between them. Edith Deen explains: "Houses of sun-dried bricks were built over the gap between the two walls. Rahab's house was in one of these strategic points, and her window looked out on the outer wall."[1] This was quite common in ancient times, where houses were often integrated into the defensive structures of a city.

On a night like any other, Rahab runs into two foreigners who strike up a conversation with her. She invites them into her home, and then things get a little awkward.

A local resident has already alerted the king of Jericho (cities had kings back then) that Rahab's guests are suspected spies scoping out his city for a possible invasion. He immediately sends messengers with orders for her to turn them in.

HARLOT WITH A HEART

Rahab intuitively discerns the unfolding situation, and in the heat of the moment, she chooses sides. **She allies herself with the spies.** Since she has heard about their powerful God and their previous exploits, Rahab has more faith in their God than in Jericho's defenses. By faith, she conceives a strategy to save her family:

* First, Rahab ushers the spies up to her roof and hides them under stalks of flax which she had previously laid out to dry.
* Next, when the king's messengers arrive, she admits the spies had been in her home, but they had already left. *"Missed 'em by that much!"*
* Then, she sends the seekers outside the city gates on a wild goose chase.
* The spies owe Rahab their lives, and she knows it.

After making sure the coast is clear, Rahab returns to her rooftop for an important and life-changing conversation with the spies. They, of course, are grateful she didn't turn them in. Rahab is focused because she knows what's coming, and she lays out her terms for helping them escape: She requires a firm commitment that her family will be spared when the invasion happens.

In this scene, Rahab is acting as the head of household. She's negotiating for the protection of a lot more people than you might realize. Her household likely includes parents, siblings, and even extended family like nieces, nephews, and maybe even servants. We can imagine Rahab will cram as many of her family members into her home as she possibly can—as long as they are willing to let Jericho fall to the Israelite warriors.

In addition to securing her family's physical protection, Rahab plays a prophetic role in the narrative. During her negotiation, Rahab prophesies:

I know that the LORD has given you the land and that dread of you has fallen on us...The LORD your God is indeed God in heaven above and on earth below. Joshua 2:9, 11b

Ruins at Ancient Jericho

A CRIMSON CORD

Recognizing her foresight and commitment to their God, the spies agree to save her family, but only if she follows their very specific instructions.

They instruct her to bind a crimson cord to her exterior window.

This way, they—and everyone with them—will know which house to avoid, because there's more to this signal than meets the eye.

Let's slow down and take a closer look at what we're reading, because this story is packed with symbolism and deeper meaning.

DIGGING DEEPER

Whenever you read narratives in the Bible, please slow down and pay close attention to what you're reading. Skimming a story or losing focus can easily lead to confusion over details.

For example, some people mistakenly assume that the spies who met Rahab were Caleb and Joshua, but this is incorrect.

Why the mix-up? There are two distinct spy stories related to the conquest of the Holy Land, each involving Israelite men sent to scout the land so they can make an informed decision about when to invade:

1. The First Spy Story (Numbers 13-14):
The Lord commands Moses to send one man from each tribe to spy out Canaan. Out of the twelve, only Joshua and Caleb are named. Joshua is from the tribe of Ephraim, and Caleb is from the tribe of Judah. They return ready to take the land, but the other ten give a negative report, resulting in their decision not to invade. The subsequent grumbling against Moses' leadership leads to the Israelites spending the next forty years "wandering" in the wilderness.

2. The Second Spy Story (Joshua 2-6):
When the time finally arrives to invade Canaan, it's Joshua who sends spies, this time just two, to scope out a specific city: Jericho. I wonder which tribe(s) they were from and why he chose only two. These are the two spies who encounter our girl Rahab, setting the stage for a pivotal moment in the Conquest.

Though they remain unnamed in the biblical text, some scholars and later traditions identify one of the spies as Salmon (from the tribe of Judah), a figure linked to significant biblical lineages, including that of King David and the promised Messiah.

THE CORD

The Hebrew word translated "cord" or "thread" in Joshua 2:21 is תקות (tik·vat), and the root of this word literally means "to bind together." Therefore, when Rahab binds the *tik·vat* to her exterior window, she is symbolically binding herself to the Israelite people and their God.

THE COLOR

The Hebrew word השני (ha·shaw·nee) is usually translated *scarlet* or *crimson*. In simpler terms, they want her to use a **RED** cord. Have you ever wondered why *red*? Taylor Swift's album hadn't come out yet, so you can scratch that one right off the top. But why not yellow? Or purple? Or blue? Or rainbow?

The spies selected red for a reason. In the Bible, and throughout history in many cultures around the world, red symbolizes blood. They make this oath:

If anyone goes out of the doors
of your house into the street,
his blood shall be on his own head...
But if a hand is laid on anyone
who is with you in the house,
his blood shall be on our head.
Joshua 2:17–19

The scarlet cord Rahab attaches to her window is a powerful symbol. It emphasizes her critical, life-or-death arrangement with the spies **and** it also holds profound significance for the Israelites who will see it.

Remember back when the Hebrews were enslaved in Egypt?

Moses, acting as God's messenger, repeatedly commanded the pharaoh to "Let my people go!" And each time he refused, a new, more devastating plague was unleashed upon the country.

The final and most severe of the ten plagues was the death of the firstborn. The Hebrews would be spared this tragedy, but only if they publicly identified themselves with the Lord by marking their door posts and lintels with the blood of an unblemished lamb or goat.

The blood would be a sign for the Destroyer to "pass over" their homes and spare their firstborn. This became an annual event to commemorate their liberation: Passover. (See Exodus 12.)

Once the connection to Passover is seen, it's impossible to unsee.

When the spies instruct Rahab to bind a scarlet cord to her exterior window as a secret code for the invading forces to "pass over" her house, every member of the Hebrew army will understand her "hidden-in-plain-sight" message:

⤷⟫⟫ **This household is bound to the God of the Hebrews.** ⟪⟪⤶

It's genius! Just imagine Joshua's leading his troops around the walled city of Jericho every day for a week, and each time they march by the window with the scarlet cord, they know exactly what it means. On the final day, they pass it SEVEN times so there is no doubt which dwelling to avoid during their fight.

Rahab is celebrated as a hero among the Israelites for her role in saving the spies, paving the way for their successful invasion. Additionally, her place as the great-great-grandmother of King David marks her as a pivotal figure in Israel's history. Her brave actions not only transformed her own life but also had a lasting impact on the lineage leading to David and the Messiah.

Additionally, unlike most of the women in the Hebrew Bible, Rahab is actually mentioned **by name** in the New Testament, **a few times:**

Side Note:
There is some debate about whether or not the "Rachab" in Matthew's genealogy is the same "Rahab" we've been learning about. Matthew spells the name with an extra letter— different than anywhere else in the Bible. There are also difficulties trying to reconcile her marriage to Salmon. The arguments are intriguing; however, common sense should prevail here if for no other reason than the text itself. Why would Matthew include a woman in Jesus' genealogy whom people have never heard of? What purpose would that serve since the rest of the genealogy includes well known men and women? It makes far more sense that Matthew includes Rahab BECAUSE people would know her story.

✢ **MATTHEW 1:5 - GENEALOGY OF JESUS**
Rahab is one of only four women mentioned in Matthew's genealogy of Jesus. (*See Side Note.*) Here she is recorded as the wife of Salmon (Was he one of the spies? Inquiring minds want to know!), and they have a son named Boaz. This means Rahab becomes Ruth's *second* mother-in-law and the great-great-grandmother of King David. AND because she is Canaanite, not Israelite, her inclusion in Jesus' genealogy is clear sign that He is a savior for all peoples. (*Read Matthew 1:5.*)

✢ **HEBREWS 11:31 - HALL OF FAITH**
In the eleventh chapter of Hebrews, the author sequentially highlights key figures from Israel's history who demonstrated their faith through their actions and responses to God's call. The chapter is often called the "hall of faith" and

showcases a lineage of faith leading up to Jesus. Rahab is one of only two of women who makes the cut. Sarah is mentioned because, despite her initial reaction of laughter, she believed God could do anything. And Rahab is included because she "received the spies with peace" (Hebrews 11:31) and did not die with the unbelievers in Jericho.

✣ **JAMES 2 - EXAMPLE OF FAITH**
In one of the Bible's most striking juxtapositions, James 2 presents Rahab **right alongside Abraham** as an example of someone "justified" or "considered righteous" by works. This concept emphasizes that true faith is evidenced by actions, meaning that genuine belief in God is demonstrated by the good deeds and righteousness of a person's life. Here, Rahab is upheld as a model of faith—a faith that shines through her brave actions of saving the spies and protecting her family.

It's also important to recognize that Rahab's prophecy the Israelites would occupy the land is fulfilled in her lifetime. She's a pretty remarkable woman.

You can read Rahab's story in **Joshua 2-6**. ✦

Personal Reflections

What stood out to you?

Did reading this chapter prompt further questions?

Look at the cover photo for this chapter and imagine why it was chosen. What do you notice?

Is there someone in your life who reminds you of **Rahab**? Someone who mustered up the courage to change her family tree? Someone who turned her back on everything she'd ever known and re-aligned her life with the Lord?

Consider sending her a quick text, encouraging message, or longer letter to let her know you're thinking of her today. Acknowledge her courage and how she inspires your walk with God.

If the woman you thought of is you, please send a message to the author at: info@valiantwomenofthebible.com so we can bear witness to your story.

NARRATIVE HISTORY OF ISRAEL
Conquest and Settlement of the Holy Land

After their exodus from Egypt and forty years of "wandering" in the wilderness, the Israelites began their official conquest of the Holy Land. This pivotal era, known as "Conquest and Settlement," saw the Israelites transition from a nomadic lifestyle to a more rooted existence in Canaan (the land promised to Abraham), where they conquered and settled the cities one by one under the leadership of Moses' successor, Joshua.

When it came time to allocate the newly conquered land, it was divided among the Twelve Tribes of Israel who were descended from Jacob's twelve sons. However, not every son of Jacob—and none of the daughters—received land. For example, the priestly tribe of Levi, were given cities and surrounding pasturelands *within the territories of the other tribes*; they possessed no "land" and were supported through offerings and gifts.

Hold the phone! This does not compute! How do we reconcile the division of land among TWELVE tribes when one of them doesn't actually receive any land?

This puzzle is solved by considering an ancient Israelite custom that honored the firstborn son and Jacob's intense love and preference for his wife Rachel. The custom entitled the eldest son to a double portion of his father's inheritance. However, Jacob deviated from this tradition by bestowing a double portion _not_ on Reuben, his firstborn son by Leah, but on Joseph, Rachel's firstborn. So, Joseph received a double portion of the inheritance; however, if you look at any map of ancient Israel, you won't see land assigned to the tribe of Joseph.

This is because Joseph's double portion was passed directly down to his two sons, Ephraim and Manasseh. Jacob symbolically adopted them as his own sons, ensuring they each received a share equal to that of their uncles, as detailed in Genesis 48. They are often referred to as "half-tribes" since together, they make up the full share of land and inheritance that would have been allotted to Joseph.

Here's a simple exercise to help you grasp how the land was divided between the Twelve Tribes of Israel, even though one tribe received no land:

- 🖐 Take 12 steps forward, representing all twelve sons of Jacob.

- 🖐 Take 1 step back for Levi since his inheritance includes no land.

- 🖐 Take 1 step back for Joseph since his inheritance is passed directly to his sons.

- 🖐 Now take 2 steps forward, one for Ephraim and one for Manasseh (Joseph's sons).

These are the 12 Tribes of Israel you'll find on maps of ancient Israel: Reuben, Gad, Simeon, Judah, Issachar, Zebulun, Asher, Dan, Naphtali, Benjamin, Ephraim, and Manasseh.

chapter eight

Sheerah

CITY BUILDER

"His daughter was Sheerah who built both
Lower and Upper Beth Horon
and Uzzen-Sheerah."
1 Chronicles 7:24

Sheerah

In our journey through the Hebrew Bible so far, we have been learning about a variety of valiant women, following the order of the books of the Bible. However, in this chapter, that changes.

So, before we delve into the life of Sheerah, let's take a moment to orient ourselves both within the historical context and the biblical text itself.

Although Sheerah's achievements are recorded in 1 Chronicles (after the Books of *Samuel* and *Kings* that we haven't yet explored), her *historical setting* is actually hundreds of years earlier. So, think of this as a type of **"literary flashback."**

Side Note:
There is some debate about where to place this story in the history of Israel because it seems like it's out of order. This is because it takes place in Canaan during the time that the Hebrews were enslaved in Egypt. If you're interested in diving deeper into this, read Professor Rabbi David Frankel's article.[1]

HISTORICAL AND GEOGRAPHICAL SETTING

Sheerah's story is set a few hundred years before the monarchy. It takes place roughly around the time of the conquest (maybe even earlier) which is why we're studying it now. She lives in the hill country of Israel, in the land of Ephraim, approximately thirteen miles north of Jerusalem. We learn about Sheerah in a genealogy.

A WORD ABOUT BIBLICAL GENEALOGIES

In ancient Israel, a person's lineage was critical to their status in society. This prompted families to maintain elaborate genealogies—many of which are in Scripture. Biblical genealogies serve a dual purpose: firstly, they unite the Israelite people by documenting their shared heritage and cultural values; and secondly, they lay the foundation for the monarchy under Saul and David.

One set of extensive genealogies comprises the first **NINE CHAPTERS** of *1 Chronicles.* These records trace the lineage of the Hebrew people starting with the first human (Adam) all the way through to the tribes of Israel who conquer and settle the land. These family trees are crucial for establishing the historical and theological foundations of the Davidic dynasty and the priesthood—they underscore the continuity and legitimacy of Israel.

1 Chronicles—where we learn about Sheerah—is rich in tribal genealogies traced almost exclusively through fathers and sons. For example:

> The **sons** of Shemida were Ahian, Shechem, Likhi, and Aniam. The **sons** of Ephraim: Shuthelah, and Bered his **son**, Tahath his **son**, Eleadah his **son**, Tahath his **son**, Zabad his **son**, Shuthelah his **son**, and Ezer and Elead.
> 1 Chronicles 7:19–21a

H O W E V E R . . .

Every once in a while, the Chronicler (author of *First* and *Second Chronicles*) inserts a short story or an interesting fact about a WOMAN into the genealogy list. 📷 And sometimes, what we learn blows gender stereotypes completely out of the water. This brings us to this chapter's woman of valor: a city builder named Sheerah.

💎 **BIBLE STUDY TIP:** It's tempting for modern readers to bypass the genealogies because they seem like irrelevant lists of names—and yes, there are a lot of unfamiliar names. However, if you treat the genealogies like maps to hidden treasures, you will find valuable nuggets buried in them.

Don't skip the genealogies. Instead, go on a treasure hunt and skim for narrative-like sentences and then pause to read them. These micro-stories, contained in as little as one verse, provide a glimpse into the lives of the people of God as they struggle to carve out a life for themselves and their families.

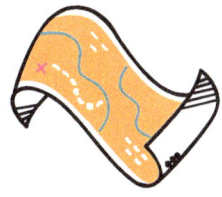

BUILDER OF CITIES

The first time we meet Sheerah is also the last time we meet Sheerah.
Sheerah is the daughter of a descendant of Ephraim (one of Joseph's sons).
Sometimes her name is spelled without the final *h*. Sheerah builds three cities
in the hill country of Ephraim: Lower Beth Horon, Upper Beth Horon, and
Uzzen-Sheerah (1 Chronicles 7:24).

 Sheerah defies gender expectations as a legit builder of cities.

In the words of Rabbi David Frankel, Associate Professor of Bible at the
Schechter Institute of Jewish Studies in Jerusalem:

> Ephraim's daughter, Sheerah is said to have built
> Upper and Lower Beit Horon. Beit Horon is one of the
> Levitical cities within the territory of Mount Ephraim
> in Joshua 21:20–22 (cf. also Joshua 16:3, 5).
> The entire family is thus living and building
> new settlements in the land.[1]

Take a moment to ponder what "building a city" entails. And then imagine a
woman trying to build one in a heavily patriarchal society. What challenges
does she face? What obstacles does she overcome?

**Here's what we know
for sure about Sheerah:**

Sheerah built three
cities, and she is noted
for this remarkable
accomplishment in a
biblical genealogy where
more than 95% of the
people remembered
are men. Please take a
moment to appreciate
this significant honor
and achievement.

UPPER & LOWER BETH-HORON

Upper and Lower Beth-Horon were located approximately 10 and 12 miles northwest of Jerusalem with a difference of about 700-800 feet elevation between the two. The cities were located on a major trade route between Gibeon and the Valley of Aiajalon and the coast. They also marked the tribal land boundaries between Benjamin and Ephraim. Lower Beth Horon was later fortified by King Solomon.

Modern Day Location of the Biblical "Upper Beth Horon"

Another interesting fact about these cities is that at least one was designated a Levitical "City of Refuge." (*See Joshua 21:22 and 1 Chronicles 6:68.*) These cities provided a safe haven for the unfortunate persons who accidentally caused the death of someone else.

 There were less than 50 cities of refuge scattered throughout the Holy Land, and Sheerah's was one of them!

Both Upper and Lower Beth-Horon as well as ***the land between them*** see a lot of action over the years. Here are a few notable battles that take place there:

* The famous battle between Joshua and five Canaanite kings, when the sun stood still (Joshua 10:6-15).

* A hieroglyphic inscription at Karnak celebrates Pharaoh Shishak's (a.k.a. Sheshonq) defeat of Beth-Horon during Rehoboam's reign over the Southern Kingdom. Rehoboam was Solomon's son. (*See next page.*)

* An attack led by Holofernes under Nebuchadnezzar in the 6th century BCE.

* A battle during the Maccabbean Revolt where Judas Maccabeus fought and killed Nicanor the Syrian in the 2nd century BCE.

IMAGINING SHEERAH

Dr. Wil Gafney, Biblical Scholar and Professor at Brite Divinity School, has spent a lot of time thinking about Sheerah. In a sermon she preached over ten years ago, inspired with sanctified imagination, Dr. Gafney describes what Sheerah's life might have been like:

She had to build her city in the right order. She couldn't start with the wallpaper and the flower arrangements. She had to start in the dirt. She had to lay her foundation. She had to build her walls and those walls had to hold – they were still at war with some of the Canaanite nations. She had to choose which buildings would be built first.

Sheerah built her own house, maybe she built a house for her mama and daddy if they were still alive. She built houses for her people and perhaps for folk she didn't even know.

And when she finished building her city, Sheerah didn't retire. She built another city. And then she built one more. Sheerah never married or gave birth. That wasn't her calling. Sheerah became the mother of cities. And her name lives on in the scriptures through her cities, the works of her hands.[2]

This sermon is fantastic. There is a link to the full transcript in the Bibliography at the back of the book, in case you'd like to read it.

HIEROGLYPHIC PROOF

The Bubastite Portal Gate, known as the "Shishak Inscription," records the military achievements of Pharaoh Sheshonq I. The relief features a list of 150+ cities he conquered during his reign. Section 2, Row 2 features the name Bat Huran (a.k.a. Beth Horon). Below is an image from a dictionary of hieroglyphics with the translation.[3]

> **Bat ḥuarn** ⟨hieroglyphs⟩
> L.D. III, 252, 24, Beth-horon; compare Heb. בֵּיתחֹרֹן (Josh. x, 10, 11), a city in Ephraim.

This showcases the city's historical significance as far back as 925 BCE!!

Left: Photo of the relief of Shoshenq I's campaign list at the Temple of Karnak, north of Luxor, Egypt.

Beit Ur al-Fauqa — Palestinian Village in the West Bank
(Upper Beth Horon)

Beit Ur al-Tahta — Palestinian Village in the West Bank
(Lower Beth Horon)

Many modern cities in the Near East are layered with history, often built directly on top of ancient cities. This fascinating practice means that beneath the bustling streets and contemporary buildings of urban landscapes lie the remnants of civilizations that have risen and fallen over thousands of years.

Originally built by Sheerah, the ancient cities of Upper and Lower Beth Horon have been linked archaeologically with two modern day Palestinian Arab villages in the West Bank: Beit Ur al-Fauqa (Upper Beth Horon) and Beit Ur al-Tahta (Lower Beth Horon). How amazing is that?! If you're interested, you can learn more about the location of the cities and view a few more recent photos on the sites listed in the image credits on page 179.

UZZEN-SHEERAH

Unfortunately, we don't know the location of the third city, Uzzen-Sheerah, as it has faded into history. However, the translation of the city's name is clearly a tribute to its builder: 'Uzzen-Sheerah' literally means 'Listen to Sheerah.' It's evident that the townsfolk respect and honor Sheerah because she is a skilled builder and knows what she's doing. We can hope that, someday, archaeologists will uncover an inscription or another artifact to help locate this ancient city. 🙏

ONE FINAL THOUGHT

Sheerah is proof that even in patriarchal ancient Israel, women were capable of building much more than family trees. **And. They. Did.**

You can read the little we know about Sheerah in <u>1 Chronicles 7:20-24</u>. ✺

Personal Reflections

What stood out to you?

Did reading this chapter prompt further questions?

Look at the cover photo for this chapter and imagine why it was chosen. What do you notice?

Is there a woman in your life who is a trailblazer and pioneer like **Sheerah**? Someone who has blown gender expectations out of the water with her career choice? Is she a minority in her field? Is she marginalized on top of it all? Has she overcome significant obstacles to succeed in her profession? Is she rocking it?

Consider sending her a quick text, encouraging message, or longer letter to let her know you're thinking of her today. Acknowledge her persistence and skill, her willingness to pave the way for others to follow in her footsteps, and/or how she is a powerful example who inspires your walk with God.

If the woman you thought of is you, please send a message to the author at: info@valiantwomenofthebible.com so we can bear witness to your story.

CAREERS WOMEN ENJOY IN MALE-DOMINATED FIELDS:

Auto Mechanic	Data Scientist	Network Architect
Aerospace Engineer	Chemical Engineer	Nuclear Engineer
Aircraft Pilot	Computer Engineer	Oil and Gas Driller
Astronaut	Judge	Physicist
Civil Engineer	Law Enforcement	Plumbing Technician
Construction Manager	Mining Engineer	Preacher
Cybersecurity Analyst	Machinist	Race Car Driver
Electrician	Marine Biologist	Software Developer
Firefighter	Mechanical Engineer	Structural Engineer
HVAC Technician	Military Officer	Welding Technician

chapter nine

Naomi, Ruth, & Orpah

DEVOTED WIDOWS

"Then they wept aloud again.
Orpah kissed her mother-in-law goodbye,
but Ruth clung to her."
Ruth 1:14

Naomi, Ruth, & Orpah

We first meet Naomi at home with her husband and two sons. They live in Bethlehem (literally "house of bread") in Judah, and the community is struggling through a horrible famine. Ironically, there's no bread in the house of bread. 🥖

Due to the overwhelming lack of food, resources, and prospects, they leave their home in Judah and migrate across the Jordan River to the region of Moab in hopes of securing a better future for their family. (*See map below for their most likely route around the Dead Sea.*)

THREE WIVES. THREE WIDOWS.

After settling in Moab, Naomi's husband dies leaving her a single mom of two in this foreign land. Naomi does the best she can to finish raising the boys on her own, and eventually each of her sons marries a Moabite woman: Mahlon marries Ruth, and Chilion, Orpah. Sadly, before either of the couples has any children, the men die.

Side Note:
Moab, located about 60 miles southeast of Bethlehem across the Dead Sea (now in modern Jordan), was named after Lot's son, born to his firstborn daughter. 🤢 Gross, I know. Ethnically, the Moabites and Israelites both trace their lineage back to Terah, Abraham's father. Despite this shared ancestry, their cultures and religions were quite distinct. Naomi's family sought refuge in Moab due to a famine in their homeland of Judah.

Although Naomi's family originally relocated to preserve their lives, that's not how things play out. Tragedy strikes, and within ten years of the move, Naomi has lost her husband and both of her sons.

Stripped of everything that gives her life meaning and security, Naomi finds herself socially vulnerable and emotionally empty. She is homesick and YEARNS for her extended family. Her old friends. Her *literal* tribe. She's experiencing all the stages of grief at once.

Then, one day while she's out working in the fields, Naomi learns that the LORD has ended the famine in Judah. She decides right then and there that it's time for her to make the long journey home to Bethlehem. Alone.

BETHLEHEM OR BUST! 🐫

Naomi is determined to make the move solo, especially since her daughters-in-law are Moabite and no longer bear any legal obligation to her. The elder widow encourages the younger widows to return home to their families of origin, remarry, and have children of their own. How will the widows respond?

In one of the most emotionally riveting scenes in the Bible, BOTH Ruth and Orpah REFUSE to leave Naomi's side.

They hug and cry and cry and hug. These three women have been through a lot together, but no matter how hard they try to reason with her, Naomi is not swayed. She sends them on their way—mothers-in-law can be stubborn sometimes, or so I've heard. 😉

Orpah reluctantly obeys Naomi's command and returns to her family of origin. Sometimes people imagine that Orpah turned her back on Naomi, but **nowhere in the text is her action judged negatively**—she's actually honoring her family by returning to them and honoring Naomi's wishes.

Ruth, however, chooses the opposite response: She resolutely refuses to leave Naomi's side, and swears a beautiful oath of loyalty to her mother-in-law:

Where you go, I will go; and where you lodge, I will lodge;
Your people shall be my people and your God my God.
Where you die, I will die, and there will I be buried.
Ruth 1:16b–17a

It's obvious Ruth is closer to Naomi than anyone else in her life, and she would much rather stay with her than return to her own family. In this way, Ruth is a maverick: She turns her back on her family, her people, her religion. She vows her undying allegiance to a foreign woman to whom she has no legal connection or moral obligation.

When Naomi realizes she's never going to talk Ruth out of her decision, she yields. Together they leave Moab and make the journey to Bethlehem. Upon arrival, their immigration statuses are immediately reversed:

> Naomi is now the native,
> and Ruth is the foreigner.

Husbandless and childless, the two women are vulnerable and unprotected. They are in desperate need, so upon arrival Ruth gets right to work. She walks to a nearby field to pick up what the harvesters left in the fields. (*See Deuteronomy 24:19-21 for an explanation of this permitted practice.*)

As Ruth gleans, she catches the eye of the wealthy land owner, a man named Boaz. He is the son of Rahab and Salmon—it's a small world, is it not?!

Once Boaz learns the new gleaning girl lives with his relative, Naomi, he instructs the harvesters to leave a little extra in the field for her.

This heartfelt concern for her well-being and display of special favor foreshadows the union to come.

When Naomi sees how much Ruth is gleaning, she is both impressed and

perplexed. When she discovers the field where Ruth has been gleaning is owned by one of her SINGLE relatives, Boaz, Naomi moves straight into matchmaker mode. Maybe *he* will become their "kinsman redeemer" and save the family from financial ruin.

Naomi compels Ruth to **secure** Boaz's affections by secretly visiting him on his threshing floor in the middle of the night. She advises her to "uncover his feet." [2,3,4] Through this "revealing," Ruth makes herself and her intentions known so Boaz has no doubt of her interest or loyalty.

MARRY ME?

In a twist reminiscent of Sadie Hawkins Day, where women propose marriage to their partners, Ruth takes bold initiative and asks Boaz to marry her.

Boaz compliments Ruth when he refers to her as an *"eshet chayil"* (literally, "woman of valor"), a phrase familiar to us from Proverbs 31:10 [5] And although he is definitely interested, he's not in a position to take action just yet. First, they must address a major obstacle to their potential union: ANOTHER kinsman redeemer—someone with the first right of refusal.

Boaz sends Ruth back home to Naomi with a generous portion of grain from the threshing floor. He then makes a bee-line to the city gate where he will have a heart-to-heart with Naomi's *closest* kinsman—the man legally obligated to purchase her land and marry Ruth to produce an heir.

Boaz brings the issue of Naomi's redemption forward in the presence of ten elders and the kinsman. As it turns out, he is ready, willing, and able to fulfill his obligation of purchasing Naomi's property. But when Boaz reminds him that this redemption also requires his marriage to the Moabitess, the man relinquishes his responsibility, clearing the way for Boaz to marry Ruth. The men seal their agreement with a sandal—an odd but meaningful tradition.

DIGGING DEEPER

In the ancient Near East, marriage was a far cry from today's romantic proposals and Pinterest-inspired weddings. Instead, marriages were strategic, orchestrated between families, tribes, and nations as a means of solidifying otherwise wobbly alliances. Romance and companionship were not required.

The union was often contingent upon a woman's ability to conceive and bear children—especially sons. Producing heirs was a necessity embedded in the economic and religious fabric of the time, and infertility was seen as a curse. Not only did it negatively impact the woman's status in her community, it also jeopardized the continuation of the family's legacy. It should come as no surprise, then, that childless widows were expected to remarry and produce a male heir, if at all possible.

This brings us back to Bethlehem where Naomi is masterfully orchestrating a surprise rendezvous for her daughter-in-love. She instructs Ruth to wash and anoint herself, dress in her best clothes, head to Boaz's threshing floor, and keep out of site—until the perfect moment. When the time is right, she should stealthily approach Boaz and uncover his "feet"[2] and "do whatever he says." Naomi's agenda is clear.

And Ruth does what she is told, up to a point; however, when Boaz startles awake, **everything changes**. Dr. Rachel Adelman convincingly argues that Boaz—instead of taking advantage of the situation—"chooses recognition over carnal knowledge."[7] He soberly asks who is there, and Ruth courageously reveals her true identity.

Then, rather than waiting for his instructions as Naomi had advised, Ruth asks Boaz to spread his robe over her—not literally, but figuratively. In a way, she's proposing marriage. Adelman observes, "*This is no simple marriage proposal...rather, it is a request to be included within the covenantal community.*"[8] Ruth is basically proposing a full-on alliance, and Boaz is both humbled and honored: He will marry her and become their kinsman redeemer.

Boaz then declares his intentions, and the elders and bystanders who witness the negotiation respond by proclaiming God's blessings on their union. 💍

> Then all the people who were at the gate, along with the elders, said, "We are witnesses. May the LORD make the woman who is coming into your house like Rachel and Leah, who together built up the house of Israel. May you produce children in Ephrathah and bestow a name in Bethlehem; and, through the children that the LORD will give you by this young woman, may your house be like the house of Perez, whom Tamar bore to Judah."
> Ruth 4:11-12 (emphasis mine)

This blessing connects Ruth, a foreigner, to these revered Hebrew women, emphasizing her potential role in fortifying the family legacy, just as Rachel did through Bilhah. Put a pin in this, because it sets up what happens next.

FIRST COMES LOVE, THEN COMES MARRIAGE, THEN COMES...

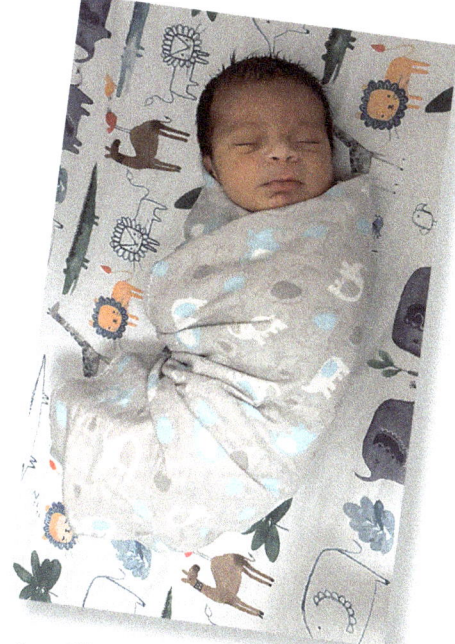

Shortly after marrying Boaz, Ruth conceives and gives birth to a son. As far as we know, she and Mahlon had no children when they were married, so this is Ruth's first child. Ruth 4:13 underscores what they already know: This baby is a gift from God.

Boaz and Ruth decide ahead of time not to name him. Instead, recognizing their firstborn as an instrument of redemption, they allow the community women to take their baby to Naomi.[6]

The women celebrate Naomi's redemption and honor the critical role her daughter-in-love has played in her life.

Declaring that **Ruth is worth more to Naomi than SEVEN sons**, the women bear witness to Ruth's extraordinary character, incredible loyalty, and the profound impact of her actions. Their words of affirmation are a form of high praise that underscore the themes of redemption, loyalty, and God's providence in this narrative.

Then, in a highly symbolic act, the women place Ruth's baby on Naomi's lap while declaring God's faithfulness: Her family line and future are secured. 📌 Her family lineage has been redeemed. As noted by Joseph Lukowski in his study of this significant event:

Side Note:
Did you notice that neither Boaz nor Ruth are present in the final scene of this story? The focus has completely shifted away from the couple and back onto the woman whose story we've followed since the beginning of the narrative: Naomi.

Obed was therefore laid on Naomi's lap in the same way that Bilhah's offspring were laid on the knees of Rachel (as proxy children), and so Naomi was the "mother" of Obed (who became the father of Jesse, who became the father of King David, whose descendant is *Ha Meschiach*—i.e., the Messiah).[9]

Once hopeless and "empty," Naomi is now redeemed and restored, seen by her community as "full" once more, with all glory given to God.[10] Together, *they* name the baby Obed which means "servant" or "worshiper" in Hebrew.

THE FAMILY LEGACY

Aside from his name and this birth narrative, the only details we know about Obed are that he grows up, starts a family, and has a son named Jesse. Jesse grows up, marries, and fathers eight boys, one of whom he names David.

This means Ruth the Moabite is the great-grandmother of King David!

Ruth is one of four women mentioned in Matthew's genealogy of Jesus, and her non-Israelite lineage is more evidence that God's plan has always included more than one people group.

You can read more about Naomi, Ruth, and Orpah in the book of <u>Ruth</u>. 🐾

Personal Reflections

What stood out to you?

Did reading this chapter prompt further questions?

Look at the cover photo for this chapter and imagine why it was chosen. What do you notice?

Is there someone in your life who reminds you of **Naomi**? Someone who endured incredible loss, but never lost her faith in God? Someone whose life has been "redeemed" in a way? A woman who has been given a new lease on life because of someone else's loving kindness towards her? Consider sending her a quick text, encouraging message, or longer letter to let her know you're thinking of her today. Acknowledge her perseverance and resilience, and share how she inspires your walk with God.

Is there someone in your life who reminds you of **Ruth**? Someone who lost her husband way too young? Someone who walked a difficult path of grief, but never gave up? A woman who found a way to support herself and make it on her own? Consider sending her a quick text, encouraging message, or longer letter to let her know you're thinking of her today. Acknowledge her tenacity and grit, and share how she inspires your walk with God.

Do you know someone who reminds you of **Orpah**? Someone whose life plans were upended by tragedy causing her to move back home, regroup, and heal so she could move forward again? Consider sending her a quick text, encouraging message, or longer letter to let her know you're thinking of her today. Acknowledge her resilience, and share how she inspires your walk with God.

If the woman you thought of is you, please send a message to the author at: <u>info@valiantwomenofthebible.com</u> so we can bear witness to your story.

Photo (left): Painting of "Bethlehem" by Cornelis de Bruijn, 1698.

NARRATIVE HISTORY OF ISRAEL

JUDGES TO MONARCHY

The historical accuracy of these durations and the sequence of the judges' rule is a subject of scholarly debate.

The book of Judges provides a glimpse into the early history of Israel after their arrival in Canaan. It offers valuable insights into their beliefs, social structures, and the challenges they faced during the nation's formative years. Regional and tribal "judges" played a pivotal role in guiding the people in matters of religion and culture.

Below is a list of known judges in the order they appear in the Bible, along with the lengths of their term, if recorded. Keep in mind that Scripture does not specify direct succession between judges:

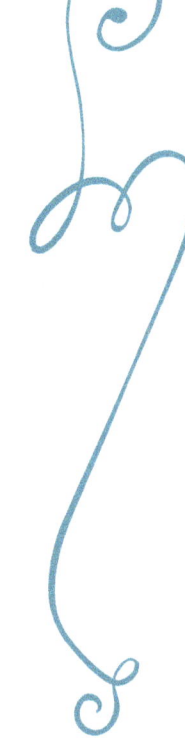

- ❖ **Othniel** - His leadership resulted in 40 years of peace (Judges 3:11).

- ❖ **Ehud** - His leadership led to 80 years of peace (Judges 3:30).

- ❖ **Shamgar** - The duration of his leadership is not specified (Judges 3:31).

- ❖ **Deborah** - Her leadership led to 40 years of peace (Judges 5:31).

- ❖ **Gideon** - His rule lasted 40 years (Judges 8:28).

- ❖ **Abimelech** - Gideon's son, who made himself king, reigned for three years, though his kingship was never widely recognized (Judges 9:22).

- ❖ **Tola** - He judged Israel for 23 years (Judges 10:2).

- ❖ **Jair** - His leadership spanned 22 years (Judges 10:3).

- ❖ **Jephthah** - He led Israel for 6 years (Judges 12:7).

- ❖ **Ibzan** - His tenure lasted 7 years (Judges 12:9).

- ❖ **Elon** - He judged Israel for 10 years (Judges 12:11).

- ❖ **Abdon** - His period of leadership was 8 years (Judges 12:14).

- ❖ **Samson** - He led Israel for 20 years (Judges 16:31).

- ❖ **Eli** - He judged Israel for 40 years (1 Samuel 4:18).

- ❖ **Samuel** - His leadership is not precisely quantified in years, but he served as both a judge and a prophet from his youth until his death (1 Sam. 7:15-17 and 25:1).

Hannah's son, Samuel, the final judge, played a crucial role in moving Israel from a theocracy to a monarchy. He anointed Saul as the first king chosen by God, ushering in a new chapter in Israel's history.

chapter ten

Deborah

PROPHET & JUDGE

"At that time Deborah, a prophet, wife of Lappidoth,
was judging Israel. She used to sit under the palm of Deborah...
and the Israelites came up to her for judgment."
Judges 4:4–5

Deborah

When we first meet Deborah, we learn that she is a prophet, a wife, and a judge over Israel—her roles are listed in that order. As the fourth judge, Deborah's leadership brings peace to Israel for a period of 40 years.

 Deborah is the only female judge and sole female military leader in the Bible.

Deborah is always easy to find. She spends a lot of time at her "outdoor office" between Ramah and Bethel in the hill country of Ephraim.

Her favorite place is under a specific tree, the 🌴 Palm of Deborah, named in her honor.

People travel from all over Israel to meet with Judge Deborah for the sole purpose of seeking her wise counsel on matters of justice.

Although we don't have the juicy details of how Deborah becomes a judge, we do know that she is "the only woman in the Bible who was placed at the height of political power by the common consent of the people."[1] She is a beloved ruler.

One day, she sends for a military leader named Barak who is living in Naphtali, west of the Sea of Galilee.

When Barak arrives, Deborah prophesies to him that (1) **God** is commanding him to prepare for battle by gathering 10,000 men from Naphtali and Zebulun; (2) that **God** will bring their enemy to the Kishon River; and (3) that **God** will give the general of the Canaanite king into his hand.

WHAT GENDER NORMS? (PART ONE)

Rather than step out in faith taking God at His word, Barak hesitates. Instead, he issues an ultimatum to Deborah:

> If you will go with me,
>
> I will go,
>
> but if you will **not** go with me,
>
> I will not go.
>
> Judges 4:8

This is an **unusual** and **unexpected** reversal of traditional gender roles.

A *man* telling a *woman* he won't go into battle *without her*?!

Just let that sit with you for a moment. Notice where this lands in your body.

Deborah agrees to accompany Barak into the battle, but first addresses his conditions.

She prophesies that because of his attitude—his lack of faith—the Lord will "sell" his opponent into the hand of a woman.

Deborah does not reveal the name of the woman who will defeat Sisera, the commander of the Canaanite army. (*Stay tuned. We'll cover this dramatic event in the next chapter.*)

Side Note:
Does this sound familiar? It reads a lot like Ruth's promise to Naomi: "Where you go, I will go." But that's where the similarity ends. Ruth pledged an oath of loyalty to Naomi. Here, Barak is literally refusing to do what Deborah asks *unless* she goes with him. It's not an oath of loyalty, it's a demand of dependency. And because of it, Barak will not be able to take any credit for defeating the army's commander.

WAKEY, WAKEY!

Deborah plays a critical role in Barak's battle plan as she is the strategist who tells him when to attack:

> Then Deborah said to Barak,
> "Up! For this is the day on which
> the Lord has given Sisera into your hand.
> Has not the Lord gone out before you?"
>
> Judges 4:14a

Deborah's remarkable strength and leadership guiding 10,000 troops to victory highlight her extraordinary capabilities as a judge and a military leader.

This remarkable achievement stands as more than just a footnote in history: It is commemorated in one of the Bible's oldest and most poetic passages, *The Song of Deborah*, a lasting tribute to a pivotal battle.

A WAR MEMORIAL FOR A WOMAN

The Song of Deborah (Judges 5) is a poetic war memorial that celebrates and honors Deborah as the sole female judge and military leader. The poem not only recounts her historic victory but also celebrates what happens when individual tribes join forces to defeat the Canaanite King Jabin while under the inspiring leadership of a woman.

The battle is recounted in poetic form so it's memorable and easily recounted from one generation to another.

The Song of Deborah is jam-packed with important details about the battle including locations, allies, and "suspects." These suspects comprise a list of Israelites who choose not to join the battle, and this leaves their loyalty in question moving forward.

The poem exposes a divided Israel as only certain tribes from west of the Jordan River unite to confront a common enemy. Notably absent were the tribes east of the Jordan, specifically Reuben and the inhabitants of Gilead (associated with the tribes of Gad and the half-tribe of Manasseh). They did not answer the call when their kinfolk were in dire need of their assistance.

The fighting itself takes place in the Valley of Jezreel at Taanach near the waters of Megiddo (a.k.a. the Kishon River). Together, the volunteer army—under the command of an amazing Ephriamite woman, Deborah, and in large part due to the cunning actions of a Kenite woman, Jael—defeats the Canaanite army under Sisera's command. (*See the next chapter for Jael's story.*)

Deborah and Jael are incredibly brave women—essential to the LORD's plan to subdue King Jabin who is utterly destroyed, thanks to this victory.

This poetic war memorial, memorized and sung for decades and eventually included in written Scripture, ensures that the people know whom to trust for help and whom to avoid for alliances.

You can read about Deborah in **Judges 4** (prose) and **Judges 5** (poetry). ✒

Personal Reflections

What stood out to you?

Did reading this chapter prompt further questions?

Look at the cover photo for this chapter and imagine why it was chosen. What do you notice?

Is there someone in your life who reminds you of **Deborah**? Someone who is a recognized leader in your community? Someone brave and committed to justice? Someone who men follow because she regularly discerns God's will and takes action?

Consider sending her a quick text, encouraging message, or longer letter to let her know you're thinking of her today. Acknowledge her leadership and influence, and share how she inspires your walk with God.

If the woman you thought of is you, please send a message to the author at: <u>info@valiantwomenofthebible.com</u> so we can bear witness to your story. Being a female leader in a patriarchal society is no joke.

Jezreel Valley with Mt. Tabor in the distance. Imagine a rain-soaked plain and it's easy to see how iron chariots were more a liability than asset to the Canaanite army during their battle with the Israelites under Deborah and Barak's command.

chapter eleven

Jael

HOST ASSASSIN

"Jael came out to meet Sisera and said to him, 'Turn aside, my lord, turn aside to me; have no fear.' So he turned aside to her into the tent, and she covered him with a rug."
Judges 4:18a

Jael

When we first meet Jael she is greeting an unexpected visitor outside her tent. She barely recognizes the man, but invites him in anyway. His name is Sisera, and he is the commander of the Canaanite army. He's oppressed the Hebrews in that region for the past **twenty years**. Until today.

In this battle, the Israelites are fighting back in a big way, and Sisera's troops are losing the battle. Which battle, you ask? The one we learned about in the last chapter—the one fought by Deborah and Barak near the Wadi Kishon, now the Kishon River. A "wadi" is a dry riverbed or valley that temporarily fills with water during seasonal rains, commonly found in desert regions.

Side Note:
The Kishon River (right), which flows near Mount Tabor, eventually reaches the Mediterranean Sea. It has various branches and tributaries, ensuring a consistent flow of water throughout the year. The land around this river, including the Jezreel Valley, is subject to heavy rains. When these downpours are intense, they can lead to a rapid increase in the river's water levels, posing a real risk of sudden and powerful flash floods.

Commanding **900 iron chariots** to enter a wadi makes sense in the DRY season, but **not** in the rainy one, and definitely not when the rain is imminent.

The torrent Kishon swept them away, the onrushing torrent, the torrent Kishon.
Judges 5:21

Unfortunately for Sisera and his army, this particular battle in this particular wadi takes place on a VERY rainy day.

MILK > WATER

Commander Sisera somehow finds his way to Jael's neighborhood. He is bloody, exhausted, afraid, and completely out of breath due to his fleeing a battle on foot. Yes, the guy in charge fled the battle and left his troops to die.

Recognizing his situation and sensing his desperation, Jael invites him to find safety in her tent. She assures him there is nothing to fear so he follows her inside.

Normally, the sight of an unrelated man entering a woman's home, particularly when she is alone, might raise concerns. But in this case, it is the *man* who is at risk.

Sisera feels safe in Jael's tent. He trusts her because his boss, King Jabin of Canaan, has peaceful relations with her husband's clan: the Kenites. Jael immediately accommodates his desire to hide, but he's really thirsty. When he requests a drink of water, the gracious host offers him milk. Why?

Dr. Tikva Frymer-Kensky, in her article about Jael in the *Jewish Women's Archive*, makes an interesting observation that Jael is "mothering" Sisera.[1] She calls our attention to Judges 5:28-30 where we get a glimpse of what Sisera's actual mother might have been thinking as she waited near the entrance of her home for his triumphant return.

> Out of the window she peered; the mother of Sisera gazed through the lattice: "Why is his chariot so long in coming? Why tarry the hoof beats of his chariots?"
> Judges 5:28

In the absence of his own mother, it's easy to imagine Sisera projecting motherly affection onto Jael as she takes on the role of nurturing protector. Reassuring Sisera that no harm will come to him, Jael tucks him in "snug as a bug in a rug"—or, in this case, ***under*** a rug.

Peeking out from under the rug, the commander instructs his host to "stand guard" outside her tent and send anyone searching for him on a wild goose chase. In this life-and-death game of hide-and-go-seek, Sisera is confident he's found a perfectly safe hiding place and falls fast asleep under Jael's rug.

But Sisera is NOT safe.

The rug is a prop serving a dual purpose in this scene: Not only is it hiding the commander from his known enemies, it's also providing cover for his host to execute her own personal plan which involves him.

Once Sisera is "fast asleep from weariness" (Judges 4:21), Jael reaches not for a mortar and pestle but for a tent peg and hammer. 🔨 Instant migraine.

> But Jael wife of Heber took a tent peg and took a hammer
> in her hand and went softly to him and drove the peg
> into his temple, until it went down into the ground—
> he was lying fast asleep from weariness—and he died.
> Judges 4:21

When Barak finally arrives at Jael's tent in pursuit of Sisera, he is surprised to learn the warrior is already dead. Jael invites him inside and reveals the commander's corpse. I'm sure Deborah's words are ringing in his ears at that moment: *"The road on which you are going will not lead to your glory, for the Lord will sell Sisera **into the hand of a woman**" (Judges 4:9).* Her prophecy is fulfilled.

WHAT GENDER NORMS? (PART TWO)

Once again, in this war story, we see traditional roles flipped on their head:

The (male) commander, Sisera, renders himself **defenseless** and **exposed** in a physically **vulnerable** position.	The (female) host, Jael, assumes a **dominant** physical stance and employs her **strength** to **quickly** dispatch his life.

This dramatic reversal of roles challenges our conventional expectations of gender dynamics, particularly in the context of ancient biblical narratives. Jael's bold and unexpected actions are shocking to those of us who were raised to believe women should always be compliant—very mindful and very demure.[2] Her behavior also raises questions about the portrayal of heroism and violence in biblical stories.

WHY HONOR JAEL?

Jael's story is not remembered purely for the historical record; it's a narrative that challenges cultural norms and delivers moral lessons about the potential within every individual to effect real change. In her article entitled, "Yael Wife of Heber the Kenite: Midrash and Aggadah," Tamar Adari explains why Jael (also spelled Yael) is generally held in a positive light:

> Yael's actions helped God to realize His plan by punishing Sisera measure for measure for his wicked deeds, and by affording Israel a military victory over their enemies.[3]

Jael's inclusion in Scripture reminds us that God often works through unlikely heroes, leading to unexpected turns of events.

Read more about Jael in **Judges 4:17-23** (prose) and **Judges 5:24-30** (poetry).

SOAPBOX MOMENT

If you're wondering why Jael's story is highlighted in this series since she murders someone, you are not alone. But would you have the same question if this were a book about valiant **men** of the Bible? Moses, Joshua, Samson, David—each of them killed at least one person.

We are simply not accustomed to reading about a **woman** taking this type of quick, brave, and physical action against another person—especially a man. Especially the commander of an army!

In a way, neither Jael's nor Deborah's stories align with how we've been conditioned to imagine the women in the Hebrew Bible. It's time we take a fresh look at the actual stories of these women and notice that they were **way stronger**, **more decisive**, and **much more powerful** than many of us may have realized.

Personal Reflections

What stood out to you?

Did reading this chapter prompt further questions?

Look at the cover photo for this chapter and imagine why it was chosen. What do you notice?

Is there someone in your life who reminds you of **Jael**? Someone who has had to make a tough choice at a pivotal moment? Someone who took difficult action to fight oppression? Someone who was able to do something others couldn't do primarily because she was in the right place at the right time—and because she did it, everything changed?

Consider sending her a quick text, encouraging message, or longer letter to let her know you're thinking of her today. Acknowledge her courage and grit, and share how she inspires your walk with God.

If the woman you thought of is you, please send a message to the author at: info@valiantwomenofthebible.com so we can bear witness to your story. Fighting oppression is not easy, and the impact it has on your life can be felt for a long, long time. As we know, the body keeps the score.

Another view of the Jezreel Valley with Mt. Tabor in the distance.

chapter twelve

Hannah

PRAYIN' MAMA

"Hannah prayed and said,
'My heart exults in the Lord;
my strength is exalted in my God.'"
1 Samuel 2:1

Hannah

When we first meet Hannah, she is at home in the hill country of Ephraim with her husband Elkanah, his other wife Peninnah, and *their* children. Hannah and Elkanah have no children of their own.

Elkanah is descended from the tribe of Ephraim and his family worships the LORD of hosts. Once a year, he takes his family on a short road trip—about 15 miles north—from their home in Ramah to the "temple" or "palace" of the Lord in Shiloh to make a **PEACE OFFERING.**

Ancient location of the temple at Shiloh

This temple was not the elaborate structure which is later built by Solomon, nor was it the portable tented Tabernacle used during the 40 years in the wilderness. Instead, it was something in between: a more permanent structure with doors, serving as a center for religious activity for 300 years.[1]

WHAT'S A "PEACE OFFERING"?

In the Hebrew Bible, the Peace Offering is one **category of sacrifices** (*see Side Note*) that includes the Thanksgiving, Freewill, and Vow offerings—remember the "vow" category for this story. These peace offerings were made with an unblemished animal and/or bread and symbolized gratitude, commitment, and unity with God.

Following the specific guidelines in *Leviticus* chapters 3-7, the priests would kill the animal and then divide it up for the sacrifice. Certain parts were wholly burnt as a tribute to God signifying His ultimate sovereignty and provision.

Then, specific parts of the animal, like the breast and right foreleg, were given to the priests to acknowledge and honor their role in the religious community.

The remaining meat was returned to the person who brought the sacrifice, usually the head of the household. This meat was intended to be shared in a communal feast that included family, friends, and servants. While the head of the household often received a significant portion, each participant would be given an equal share, underscoring the spirit of the gathering as one of community and fellowship.

This communal aspect of the peace offering was intended to symbolically remind the participants of their connection to each other and to God.

Ironically, it's at Elkanah's family meal following their **peace** offering where we see just how complex and challenging family relationships can be—especially when polygamy and infertility come to dinner. This echoes some of the same tensions we've witnessed earlier in Israel's history between Rachel and Leah. (*See Chapter 4: "Rachel & Leah, Sister Wives."*)

PERNICIOUS PENINNAH

When Elkanah receives back his portion of meat from the priest, instead of dividing the portions equally between himself, his two wives, his sons and daughters, he deliberately gives his wife Hannah a double portion.

Unfortunately for everyone present, this pity-full gesture backfires. Not only does Hannah become even more self-conscious of her "closed womb," Peninnah—who never misses the chance to embarrass her barren counterpart—seizes the opportunity to shame her in front of everyone. She is a quintessential "mean girl." 😈

Peninnah's perpetual harassment of Hannah has taken a huge toll, and it becomes too much: she bursts into tears and refuses to eat. Immediately, in typical hubby "fix-it" fashion, Elkanah rushes to the rescue saying, "But, Babe! You've got **ME**! Am I not worth more to you than ten sons?" 😂 (No comment.)

As soon as the meal ends, Hannah excuses herself and makes a bee-line for the temple to pray. She walks right past Eli the Priest who is seated near the entrance. Ignoring him, she enters the outer court.

This tormented soul brings her whole, authentic self to the LORD of Hosts through prayer in quiet solitude. She cries out to the only One who will understand her pain.

She was deeply distressed and prayed to the LORD and wept bitterly. She made this vow:

"O Lord of hosts, if only you will look on the misery of your servant and remember me and not forget your servant but will give to your servant a male child, then I will set him before you as a nazirite until the day of his death. He shall drink neither wine nor intoxicants, and no razor shall touch his head."

...She was speaking in her heart; only her lips moved, and her voice was not heard.
1 Samuel 1:10–11, 13a

Hannah is clearly a woman of deep, personal faith who believes in a God who still performs miracles.

ABOUT HANNAH'S VOW

Hannah's private, personal vow to the LORD is that, if He would **GIVE** her a baby boy, she would **GIVE** him back to the LORD, and he would be a Nazirite. (*See Side Note on page 95.*) The repeated use of the same Hebrew verb for "give" emphasizes the sacred act of offering what is received from God back to Him in devotion.

Additionally, Hannah's pledge holds particular significance due to its timing and nature:

🕐 **Smart Timing:** Hannah chooses to make her vow during her family's peace offering, a ceremonial time when vows are traditionally made. This moment underscores the depth of her faith and her commitment to dedicate her son to the Lord's service.

🤎 **Bold Nature:** Hannah specifically prays for a son, not a daughter, intending to dedicate him to full-time temple service. Such a vow, especially from an infertile woman, is bold and unusual but not unprecedented, even in modern times. The boldness of her promise is highlighted by the fact that, as a married woman under biblical law, she technically does not have the authority to make such a vow independently (*See Numbers 30:6-15*). When it all comes down, the final decision is Elkanah's. What will he say?

MISJUDGED MOURNING

The entire time Hannah is praying, she is closely watched—and judged—by the priest she had passed earlier. He can see her lips moving, but hears nothing, so something is "off," right?

The priest makes an incorrect assumption: This woman must have had too much to drink at the family feast! He is completely offended on God's behalf and interrupts her prayer, accusing her of making a "drunken spectacle" of herself (1 Samuel 1:14).

How do you think Hannah feels in this moment? Afraid? Misunderstood? Ashamed? Judged? Something else?

Startled, Hannah soberly explains:

I have drunk neither wine nor strong drink, but I have been pouring out my soul before the LORD... I have been speaking out of my great anxiety and vexation.
1 Samuel 1:15–16

How do you think Eli feels in this moment? Guilty? Embarrassed? Ashamed? Convicted? Something else?

Although the priest does not apologize for his mistake, he *does* bless Hannah interceding on her behalf and asking the Lord to grant her request. Little does Eli know, **he himself will be the one to raise the baby for whom he just prayed.**

Once their time at the temple has concluded, Elkanah's family returns home to the hill country of Ephraim. The couple gets busy, and Hannah conceives. Nine months later, she gives birth to a baby boy whom they name "Samuel" which literally means "God has heard."

As noted earlier, Hannah's vow to give her son over to full-time service at the temple depends on her husband's approval. Although we have no idea how, when, or where she explains her vow to Elkanah, it's refreshing to observe Hannah's husband fully supporting his wife's vow to the Lord and her plan for their only son. (*Read 1 Samuel 1:21-23.*)

HANNAH'S PRAYER

At some point after Samuel's birth, Hannah offers a prayer of thanksgiving to the Lord. Her prayer, recorded in 1 Samuel 2:1-10 (*included on page 101*), parallels and foreshadows other prayers in the Scriptures, notably *The Magnificat* of Mary in *Luke*. Both prayers reflect themes of exaltation of the lowly, divine justice, and the fulfillment of God's promises.

Side Note:
Hannah's prayer is still recited annually on the first day of *Rosh Hashanah*. This inclusion underscores the prayer's significance as a powerful expression of hope, faith, and divine intervention, aligning well with the reflective and introspective nature of the New Year celebrations in Judaism.

In her prayer, Hannah thanks God for giving her a son, and declares His sovereignty, power, and justice. It is a beautiful expression of praise and thanksgiving, and a testimony to the power of prayer and faith.

> There is no Holy One like the LORD, no one besides you; there is no Rock like our God.
> 1 Samuel 2:2

This ancient prayer is packed with Parallelism, a poetic form used throughout the Hebrew Bible—particularly in the wisdom literature like *Psalms* and *Proverbs*—to emphasize key themes. (*See "Digging Deeper" on the next page.*)

DIGGING DEEPER

I'd like to introduce you to a distinctive and meaningful poetic structure found throughout the Hebrew Bible: PARALLELISM. It is easy to spot in the *Psalms*, *Proverbs*, and prophets—and right here in 1 Samuel. 😊

Hebrew Parallelism is a literary technique in which a single thought is expressed in more than one way in consecutive lines, where each line or phrase reinforces, contrasts, or further develops the idea presented in the first. Parallelism in the Hebrew Bible can take various forms:

- ❖ Synonymous: The second line or clause restates the idea of the first in different words or clauses.

- ❖ Antithetical: The second line or clause presents a contrasting idea.

- ❖ Synthetic (or Constructive): The second line or clause adds further information or completes the thought of the first.

- ❖ Chiastic: The structure mirrors itself around a central theme, often in an A-B-B-A pattern, emphasizing the depth and centrality of the core idea. (*Bonus: If you draw lines to connect the matching clauses, the pattern creates an "X" which is "chi" in Greek.*)

The writers of the Hebrew Bible were inspired to use this type of poetic expression to enhance the beauty of the text, make it easy to memorize, and deepen our understanding of the text by embedding key concepts through repetition and contrast.

1 Samuel 1:25 is a great example of "Synthetic Parallelism" where the second clause builds upon the first to open our eyes to see what's really going on. The structure of the verse is straightforward, using two main clauses connected by "and," which links the actions together, emphasizing that they are parts of a single religious act.

They | slaughtered | a bull *and* They | brought | the child to Eli.

These parallel clauses emphasize that EACH of these actions is an offering to the Lord, with the child's presentation being particularly significant. Each clause contributes equally to the overall meaning, reinforcing the gravity of the commitment being made by Hannah and her family. Interesting, right?!

A Theory about Samuel's Age When He Moved to Shiloh

When Hannah prayed to God for a son, she vowed to "give him back" to the Lord for a life of service.

We know that Hannah waited until she had weaned Samuel before taking him to Eli at the temple in Shiloh. At that time, he was described as "young." The term in Hebrew could imply an age anywhere from toddler to teenager.

As you might imagine, there are numerous theories about how old Samuel was when he was transferred into Eli's guardianship. I'd like to add my own theory to the mix: I think Samuel was three years old at the time.

My theory finds support in the specific sacrifice made by Hannah and Elkanah—the offering of a three-year-old bull—as part of fulfilling their vow. (*Refer to the Side Note on page 99 and "Digging Deeper" on page 97 for supporting evidence.*)

I believe the bull was intentionally chosen to mirror Samuel's age and symbolize their gratitude for the initial, formative years they enjoyed with their miracle baby.

This time allowed for essential bonding and nurturing (and potty training) critical to his early development.

The choice of a young bull likely represents the completion of this nurturing phase with his parents and Hannah's commitment to honor her vow to the Lord.

BONDING TIME

After Samuel is born, Hannah decides to skip the annual family trip to Shiloh, choosing instead to stay home with the baby until he is weaned. When it's time to fulfill her vow, Hannah, likely accompanied by her husband Elkanah, takes Samuel to Shiloh to make an offering. (*See the spotlight article on the previous page for more details.*)

They pack up the family and all the necessary supplies for their offering, including a three-year-old bull, some flour, and wine. However, it's crucial to clarify: Their **VOW** offering is neither the animal, the flour, nor the wine.

The true offering to fulfill Hannah's vow is <u>her only son</u>, Samuel, who will spend the rest of his life in service to the Lord.

Side Note:
The number of many bulls Hannah takes to Shiloh is debated due to a text variation in 1 Samuel 1:24. So, let's get curious explore!

<u>King James Version:</u>
"And when she had weaned him, she took him up with her, with three bullocks [bulls]..."

<u>New Revised Standard Version:</u>
"When she had weaned him, she took him up with her, along with a three-year-old bull..."

The Masoretic Text (a Hebrew manuscript dating to the 9th century AD) records Hannah taking <u>three bulls</u> to Shiloh; however, the most ancient manuscripts of 1 Samuel mention only <u>one bull</u>:

(1) Septuagint (LXX) Greek manuscript of 1 Samuel dates to the 4th and 5th centuries AD

(2) 4Q Samuel[a] (Dead Sea Scrolls) dates to 50-25 BCE

Since the two oldest manuscripts match (LXX and 4Q Samuel[a]), and **ALL** the manuscripts record **only one bull slaughtered** in 1 Samuel 1:25, it's easy to see why most scholars accept "a three-year-old bull" as the original reading.

It's important to note that Hannah does not abandon her son at the temple. **She continues to actively participate in his life**, marking each visit with a tangible symbol of her love.

HOMEMADE "LITTLE ROBES" FOR SAMUEL

Hannah's deep faith and the experience of motherhood has transformed her. She is now known at the temple as "Samuel's mom," and she never shows up empty-handed. At least once a year, she brings a new "little robe" that she's made for Samuel and gifts it to him in person.

The story about Hannah wraps up the way it started, with a family road trip to Shiloh. We are reminded yet again that Elkanah faithfully takes his family to the temple at Shiloh every year to make a peace offering. He brings both wives and all the kiddos—but things are definitely different now.

Eli is so impressed with Hannah that he regularly prays God will bless her with more children. In time, the couple has three more sons and two daughters—five younger siblings for Samuel. They definitely need a bigger table at the communal feast. 😊

Hannah's story is a profound testament to the courage and faith of a woman who, in the face of deep personal pain and societal pressure, finds strength in her own relationship with God. Not only does she make a vow to the Lord, she keeps it. And that baby she prayed for on that awful night in Shiloh all those years ago grows up to become a pivotal figure in Israel's history serving as prophet, judge, and anointer of kings.

This is a powerful reminder that one person's faith and determination can impact not only their immediate family but also future generations and potentially alter the course of history.

You can read Hannah's story in 1 Samuel 1-2. 🖋

Personal Reflections

What stood out to you?

Did reading this chapter prompt further questions?

Look at the cover photo for this chapter and imagine why it was chosen. What do you notice?

Is there a woman in your life who, like **Hannah**, has faced personal despair or societal pressure with remarkable resilience and courage? Someone who has made significant sacrifices for the well-being of her children? Think of someone whose story of perseverance, faith, and the fulfillment of a long-held desire has not only shaped her own journey but also inspired those around her.

Consider sending her a quick text, encouraging message, or longer letter to let her know you're thinking of her today. Acknowledge her strength, faith, and/or share how she inspires your walk with God.

If the woman you thought of is you, please send a message to the author at: info@valiantwomenofthebible.com so we can bear witness to your story. The struggles are real.

HANNAH'S PRAYER ~ 1 SAMUEL 2:1-10

1 Hannah prayed and said,
  "My heart exults in the Lord;
  my strength is exalted in my God.

  My mouth derides my enemies
  because I rejoice in your victory.

2 There is no Holy One like the Lord,
  no one besides you;
  there is no Rock like our God.

3 Talk no more so very proudly;
  let not arrogance come from your mouth,
  for the Lord is a God of knowledge,
  and by him actions are weighed.

4 The bows of the mighty are broken,
  but the feeble gird on strength.

5 Those who were full have hired
  themselves out for bread,
  but those who were hungry are fat with spoil.
  The barren has borne seven,
  but she who has many children is forlorn.

6 The Lord kills and brings to life;
  he brings down to Sheol and raises up.

7 The Lord makes poor and makes rich;
  he brings low; he also exalts.

8 He raises up the poor from the dust;
  he lifts the needy from the ash heap
  to make them sit with princes
  and inherit a seat of honor.
  For the pillars of the earth are the Lord's,
  and on them he has set the world.

9 He will guard the feet of his faithful ones,
  but the wicked will perish in darkness,
  for not by might does one prevail.

10 The Lord! His adversaries will be shattered;
  the Most High will thunder in heaven.

  The Lord will judge the ends of the earth;
  he will give strength to his king
  and exalt the power of his anointed."

**What types of Hebrew parallelism
do you notice in this prayer?**

**How does the parallelism impact your
understanding of this passage?**

SIMPLE TIMELINE OF ISRAEL'S HISTORY
c. 1050 BCE – 500 BCE

This **timeline** includes some of the most recognized and significant events and figures during this period. *Some of the exact dates and figures are subject to scholarly debate. "c." is short for "circa" which means "around."*

c. 1050-1010 BCE
- Reign of King Saul, the first king of Israel.

c. 1010-970 BCE
- Reign of King David, who establishes Jerusalem as the capital and unifies the tribes of Israel.

c. 970-931 BCE
- Reign of King Solomon, who builds the first Temple in Jerusalem: "Solomon's Temple."

931 BCE
- The united kingdom of Israel splits in two after Solomon's death: the Northern Kingdom of Israel and the Southern Kingdom of Judah.

c. 875-853 BCE
- Reign of King Ahab of Israel, notable for his confrontations with the prophet Elijah.

722/721 BCE
- Fall of Samaria (capital city) to the Assyrian Empire and the end of the N. Kingdom of Israel, leading to the deportation of many Israelites.

c. 715-687 BCE
- Reign of King Hezekiah of Judah, noted for religious reforms and for withstanding the Assyrian siege of Jerusalem.

c. 640-609 BCE
- Reign of King Josiah of Judah, who enacts major religious reforms and finds the "Book of the Law" in the Temple, as recounted in I Kings 22.

630 BCE - 620 BCE
- Period of the late monarchic Judah.
- Prophet Nahum prophesies against Nineveh.

612 BCE
- Fall of Nineveh, capital of the Assyrian Empire, which leads to a power vacuum in the region.

609 BCE
- Death of King Josiah of Judah during a battle against Pharaoh Necho II of Egypt at Megiddo.
- Prophet Zephaniah active around this time.

605 BCE
- The Battle of Carchemish: Babylonian victory over Egypt and Assyria. Rise of the Neo-Babylonian Empire under Nebuchadnezzar II.

597 BCE
- First Babylonian conquest of Jerusalem.
- Jehoiachin, King of Judah, is deported to Babylon.
- Prophet Ezekiel among the first batch of exiles.

587/586 BCE
- Second Babylonian conquest of Jerusalem.
- Looting and destruction of Solomon's Temple.
- King Zedekiah is captured and Jerusalem is razed.
- Major deportation of Jews to Babylon.
- Prophet Jeremiah active during this period.

539 BCE
- Fall of Babylon to Cyrus the Great of Persia.
- Beginning of the Persian period.

538 BCE
- Cyrus the Great issues a decree allowing Jews to return to Jerusalem and rebuild the Temple.
- First wave of exiles return to Jerusalem under the leadership of Sheshbazzar and later Zerubbabel.

536 BCE
- The foundation for the Second Temple is laid in Jerusalem.

520 BCE - 515 BCE
- The Second Temple in Jerusalem is completed under the leadership of Governor Zerubbabel.
- Prophets Haggai and Zechariah active during this period, encouraging the rebuilding of the Second Temple (a.k.a. Zerubbabel's Temple).

chapter thirteen

Bathsheba

BEAUTY. QUEEN.

"Then Bathsheba bowed with her face to the ground
and did obeisance to the king and said,
'May my lord King David live forever.'"
1 Kings 1:31

Bathsheba

When we first meet Bathsheba (Hebrew for "Daughter of Abundance"[1]), she is at her home in Jerusalem—alone. Her husband, Uriah the Hittite, is away.

MEANWHILE, IN THE CITY OF DAVID...

While his officers and "Mighty Men" (an elite group of warriors including Bathsheba's husband) are out of town fighting battles with neighboring nations, King David is relaxing at the royal residence in the oldest part of Jerusalem. One afternoon, he takes a stroll up to his rooftop to enjoy the view of his territory.

At this time, rooftops are flat and perfectly suited for socializing, relaxation, and thinking. Maybe David is imagining his men winning the battles they are currently fighting, or maybe he's reminiscing about his own past—about the giant he killed when he was a child or Israel's first King he used to entertain with his harp playing or his dear friend Jonathan who died in their youth.

As King David allows his mind to wonder, he also allows his eyes to wander. It's not long until he spots a beautiful woman bathing. As far as we know, she is completely unaware that she is being watched.

✦ **SOMETHING TO NOTICE:**

In 2 Samuel 11-12, Bathsheba is portrayed as a **passive** participant.[2] She is mentioned by name **only once** when she is identified as the "daughter of Eliam, the wife of Uriah the Hittite." Everywhere else, she is referred to as "the woman" or "Uriah's wife." This is an **intentional**, inspired decision to highlight her **passivity** and **innocence** in this unfolding scenario.

SEDUCTRESS OR SURVIVOR?

Some Bible teachers irresponsibly promote a weak theory that Bathsheba is a seductress who strategically selects an immodest, obvious spot to bathe **on *her* roof** in order to catch the King's eye—but **IT'S NOT TRUE!**

The fact is, the passage contains absolutely no mention or hint of *where* in her home she is bathing.

> It happened, late one afternoon when David rose <u>from his couch</u> and was walking about on the roof of the king's house, that he saw from the roof a woman bathing; the woman was very beautiful.
> 2 Samuel 11:2

What is undeniable and beyond any shadow of a doubt is the *King's* vantage point. He is on *his* rooftop, and *from there* he can see into the homes near the palace. Rather than avert his gaze, David fixates on the woman, and decides he must have her for himself.

He can't stop thinking about her and asks who she is. As readers, we might assume that once he learns she is married, he will leave her alone. However, that's not what happens. His inquiry proves to be pointless, as it has zero impact on his decision. 😟

When King David learns the woman is the **wife** of one of his 37 Mighty Men and the **granddaughter** of one of his most trusted advisors, he is confronted with a clear choice: Is he a loyal leader or a selfish tyrant? Does he deny himself or indulge himself? After all, he is the King!

We have no idea how long he weighs the pros and cons, but tragically for everyone involved, he decides to take advantage of the situation. Armed with insider knowledge that her husband is out of town for a while, the King summons Uriah's wife to the palace. **DOES SHE HAVE A CHOICE?**

As indicated in the text, it is crystal clear that the King summons the woman for one reason and one reason only. And though we're given no details of their encounter, we learn that David has his way with her. After this encounter, the Hebrew text indicates Uriah's wife cleaned up and returned to her own home.[3] (*See Side Note on page 106.*)

Bathsheba arrives home to process what just happened. Alone. Violated. Confused. A few weeks later, when her period never arrives, she realizes she is pregnant, and there is only one man who could be the father: King David.

When Bathsheba sends word to the King about her pregnancy, he is mortified. What will people say? What will his troops say? It's clear David has no intention of an ongoing relationship with her, because he hastily hatches a plan to cover it up.

PLAN A: BRING HIM HOME

King David pulls out all the stops and recalls Bathsheba's husband from the battlefield to Jerusalem. His plan is simple: Bring Uriah home, and he will naturally spend the night with his beautiful wife, thereby covering up David's sin and protecting Bathsheba from public disgrace.

Side Note:
This part of Bathsheba's story is detailed in 2 Samuel 11. Some English translations (e.g., NRSV, NAB, NLT) appear to blend two separate cleansing events into one, introducing a concept not found in the original Hebrew or its Greek translation (Septuagint, or LXX). For clarity: Verse 2 depicts Bathsheba taking a literal bath, while verse 4 describes a separate cleansing after her encounter with King David—a purification ritual unrelated to her menstrual cycle. Therefore, if your translation includes "monthly," "cycle," or "period," please know these are interpretive additions. Leaving out these details does not change the fundamental narrative.[4]

Only one problem: When Uriah arrives in Jerusalem, he doesn't go home.

It's like a coach in the Super Bowl trying to test a key player's dedication by urging him to leave at halftime to be with his wife. Despite the temptation, a committed player stays focused on the game, knowing he can return to his wife afterward.

Similarly, Uriah, fully focused on his duties, resists all temptations, even when David attempts to facilitate the encounter by getting him drunk.

Uriah refuses to go home each night he's in town.

That's how a mighty warrior's brain works and how a selfish king's plan fails. I wonder if he has picked up on something.

PLAN B: BURY HIM

The King decides that the only way to conceal his crime is to get rid of Bathsheba's husband. He sends top secret orders to Uriah's commanding officer, who conveniently happens to be David's nephew. The instructions are clear:

In the letter he wrote, "Set Uriah in the forefront of the hardest fighting, and then draw back from him, so that he may be struck down and die."
2 Samuel 11:14

This time, David's plan works. Uriah is killed in battle. As you might imagine, when Bathsheba hears the news, she is devastated and enters into a time of mourning for her fallen husband. She remains completely oblivious that David orchestrated the whole thing.

As soon as her time of mourning is completed, King David sends for Uriah's pregnant widow, moves her into his palace, and makes her his **FOURTH** wife. As Tikva Frymer-Kensky observes, King David has a habit of collecting other men's wives,[5] progressively becoming more brazen with each acquisition.[6]

DOES SHE HAVE A CHOICE?

At this point in the narrative, David thinks he has everything under control, confident that his secret sin will remain undiscovered. Within the palace, several individuals are aware of different aspects of his actions, yet no single person holds all the pieces of the puzzle.

Some have noted David's interest in Bathsheba, while others are aware of his attempts to bring Uriah home. None, however, know about the deadly instructions in the letter sent to Joab, nor are they aware that Bathsheba is carrying David's child. On the battlefield, although Joab executes the King's command, he is clueless about the reasons behind it. Thus, despite numerous clues, no one has enough information to piece together the full extent of what is unfolding.

EXCEPT GOD.

God sees every hidden deed and, in response, sends the prophet Nathan to confront the King. Granted an audience, Nathan opts not to confront David directly but instead tells a story about a profound injustice that ignites his anger. Once King David declares that the villain in his story deserves death,

Nathan delivers a divine rebuke with resounding clarity (2 Samuel 12:7-12), exposing David as the true perpetrator of the crime: **YOU** ARE THE MAN!

The prophet confronts the King about his abuse of power, his coercion of Bathsheba, and the murder of her innocent husband. By exposing these severe ethical and moral breaches, Nathan reminds David that even though he is the anointed King of Israel, he is still subject to the Law of Moses—a law he has blatantly violated through his acts of adultery and murder.

When David realizes that he has sinned not just against Bathsheba and Uriah but also against the Lord, he sincerely repents. Psalm 51 records his prayer of contrition: *"Create in me a clean heart, O God..."* But repentance rarely changes consequences—and this time, the consequences are severe. Their child is struck with a serious illness and dies seven days later. (*See "Digging Deeper" on page 110 for further reflection on this difficult passage.*)

> 📌 **SOMETHING ELSE TO NOTICE:**
>
> This is another signal that Bathsheba is not responsible for her pregnancy. As Jo Ann Hackett observes, *"The narrative does not seem to hold her responsible for her actions with David, and the punishment that is meted out, that their child should die, is aimed by YHWH and Nathan at David, **not** Bathsheba."*[7] It turns out, **this is about him, *not* her**.

Although the child's age at the time he becomes ill is not specified, tradition holds that the boy died a week after his birth. This timing suggests that he might not have received his name yet, as names were often given on the eighth day during the circumcision ceremony.

GOING THROUGH THE UNIMAGINABLE

In less than one year, Bathsheba experiences a whirlwind of life-changing events. She goes from being married to an elite Hittite warrior to being violated by the king; from being the wife of one to becoming "one of the wives"; from being a first-time mom to becoming a grieving parent.

The King is profoundly impacted by the unexpected death of the baby, feeling a deep sense of responsibility for the tragic loss. This shared, unimaginable grief not only softens but also strengthens the marital bond between him and Bathsheba, setting it apart from his relationships with his other current (and future) wives.

From this point forward, Bathsheba is referred to as "David's wife." Together, they build a strategic partnership that lasts the rest of their lives. And despite the difficult circumstances that brought her to the King's palace, she eventually finds peace there.

A while later, Bathsheba conceives again—this time, the circumstances are completely different. She delivers a healthy baby boy who enjoys a very long life and grows up to be considered one of the greatest kings and wisest rulers in all of Israel's history: King Solomon. Over the years, she bears him several more children, including a son they name Nathan. *(Do you think they named him after the prophet?)*

⏩ FAST FORWARD A FEW DECADES

As David's health is in decline, Bathsheba, who has been notably absent from the story, re-emerges as a force to be reckoned with. 💪🏽❤️

Her longtime ally, the prophet Nathan, has brought news that the son of one of David's *other* wives has declared himself King without his knowledge or blessing. Nathan and Bathsheba know that if her son, Solomon, is not crowned king, they will all be killed—that's how things often went down in those days.

Though some would have fled the palace in fear for their lives, Bathsheba rises to the occasion and takes a stand for herself and her family. She and Nathan agree on a plan to preserve their lives and secure David's legacy.

They decide SHE should go in first. And she does. She's a confident woman.

Even though the elderly and feeble King is being attended by a newer and younger wife, Bathsheba confidently enters the room, bows before him, and shows her husband deep respect.

Quickly bringing him up to date on the usurpation of his throne by one of his sons from another wife, she gently reminds the King of **HIS** solemn promise to her—*I wonder when he made it.* 🤔

> She said to him, "My lord, you swore to your
> maidservant by the LORD your God, saying,
> 'YOUR son Solomon shall succeed me as king,
> and HE shall sit on my throne.'"
> 1 Kings 1:17 (emphasis mine)

DIGGING DEEPER

The story in 2 Samuel 12 is particularly challenging! Much ink has been spilled and many keyboards worn out by scholars attempting to explain why David was not condemned to death for his actions and why his child had to die. Most explanations are well-researched and logical, aligning their conclusions with what we know of God's character.[8] Others, not so much.

Rather than focus on David's transformation, let's focus our attention on how this situation likely impacted Bathsheba. As you know, she has been portrayed as a passive participant in this narrative. It almost feels like what's happening to her is a side note—as if she's merely a pawn in someone else's story. That HER story doesn't matter. But it's not true.

Bathsheba was impregnated by the King of Israel, and while expecting, her husband was tragically (and strategically) killed in battle. Initially a victim of circumstances beyond her control, she carried the king's baby to full term and gave birth to a healthy boy. Although we don't know how long the boy lived before falling ill, we know his sickness lasted seven days and ended in death.

The number seven, deeply embedded in biblical stories and teachings, symbolizes fullness, perfection, and the completion of God's plans. In this context, I believe it marks the end of Bathsheba's passivity. Emerging from this devastating period transformed, it is this resilient woman who raises the boy who will become one of Israel's greatest and wisest kings.

Bathsheba's journey from a silent figure overshadowed by the actions of others to a proactive and influential matriarch showcases her remarkable adaptability and strength. Her active role in ensuring her son Solomon's ascension to the throne is a testament to her strategic thinking and well-honed assertiveness. This transformation highlights not only her survival but her ability to thrive and shape the legacy of the Davidic line.

No longer the passive figure we once knew, Bathsheba now boldly presses her husband to keep his promise and appoint **their** eldest son, Solomon, as his "co-regent." Together, they could rule side-by-side until David's passing.

Eventually, Nathan enters the room and confirms Bathsheba's words. The prophet reassures King David that taking this action now will enable Solomon's smooth succession to the throne in the future.

Notice that it is Bathsheba's fervent advocacy, combined with the Nathan's corroboration of her claims, that ultimately secures Solomon's position as the future King of Israel—a role he might never have ascended to without her timely and direct intervention on his behalf. And with that, Bathsheba quietly recedes into the background, her pivotal role in shaping the future of the Davidic Dynasty complete.

Bathsheba is one of four women listed in Matthew's genealogy of Jesus, though unnamed. She is simply recorded as "the wife of Uriah" (Matthew 1:6), a not-so-subtle reminder that the skeleton's in Jesus' family tree included a royal scandal worthy of its own feature film.

You can learn more about Bathsheba in 2 Samuel 11-12 and 1 Kings 1-2. ☙

Artist's Rendering of the Temple Built by King Solomon

Bonus Info: Solomon eventually inherits his father's throne and oversees the construction of the Temple in Jerusalem. When it's completed around 957 BCE, **Solomon's Temple** instantly becomes a the spiritual center for worshipers of the LORD and a symbol of Israel's national identity. The temple is renowned for its stunning architecture and lavish decorations.

Personal Reflections

What stood out to you?

Did reading this chapter prompt further questions?

Look at the cover photo for this chapter and imagine why it was chosen. What do you notice?

Is there a woman in your life who, like **Bathsheba**, has suffered through tremendous loss? Someone who had to overcome difficult circumstances brought on her due to the actions of other people? Someone who found a way to create a meaningful life for herself despite the challenges she faced along the way? Or someone who has really become quite the advocate for her children?

Consider sending her a quick text, encouraging message, or longer letter to let her know you're thinking of her today. Acknowledge her courage, tenacity, resilience, advocacy, and/or share how she inspires your walk with God.

If the woman you thought of is you, please send a message to the author at: info@valiantwomenofthebible.com so we can bear witness to your story.

 # THE TEL DAN STELE (732 BCE)

Discovered in 1993 at Tel Dan in northern Israel (near the Golan Heights), this stele is an important artifact for the field of biblical archaeology. (See page 50 for the definition of "stele.")

The broken fragment pictured here references the "house of David" as a dynastic and geopolitical entity.[9]

The inscription as a whole provides extrabiblical proof that David not only existed, he also founded a dynasty in Judah.[10]

chapter fourteen

Jehosheba

PRINCE PROTECTOR

"Thus she hid him from Athaliah,
so that he was not killed."
2 Kings 11:2

Jehosheba

When we first meet Jehosheba, she is sneaking around the palace in Jerusalem, but it's no longer David's palace. Approximately **125 years have passed** since David was king over Israel, and the palace now belongs to one of his descendants—except, he just died. When his mom learns of his death, she determines to seize the throne for herself, and it's a bloody mess—literally.

Our story opens in the Southern Kingdom of Judah with the Queen Mother on a murderous rampage killing all potential heirs to the throne, and our girl Jehosheba is on a mission to save the baby prince.

HISTORICAL CONTEXT

The setting of Jehosheba's story requires a lot more historical context than others, and it's important for responsible interpretation. Here's a brief overview of the events in Israel's history that bring us to Jehosheba's story:

Think back to when the Israelites conquered the Holy Land. Around that time, the Hebrews were ruled by judges like Deborah and Gideon who, under God's guidance, provided administrative and military leadership. After a few hundred years of this, the people of Israel decided it was time for a change: They demanded a king so they could be like other nations.

As you can imagine, it would take a special type of leader to help transition the people from the rule of judges to centralized rule under a king. And guess who it was? It was Hannah's son, Samuel! The miracle baby for whom she prayed at the temple in Shiloh—the boy she later dedicated to the Lord's service—grew into the man who served as Israel's the final Judge. In fact, it was Samuel who anointed Israel's first two kings: Saul and David.

King David was revered in Israel's history as a great warrior, a prolific writer of Psalms, and a respected leader. He's also notorious for his coercion of Uriah's wife and unprovoked murder of her husband.

THE GENEALOGIES OF THE
KINGS
OF ANCIENT ISRAEL AND JUDAH

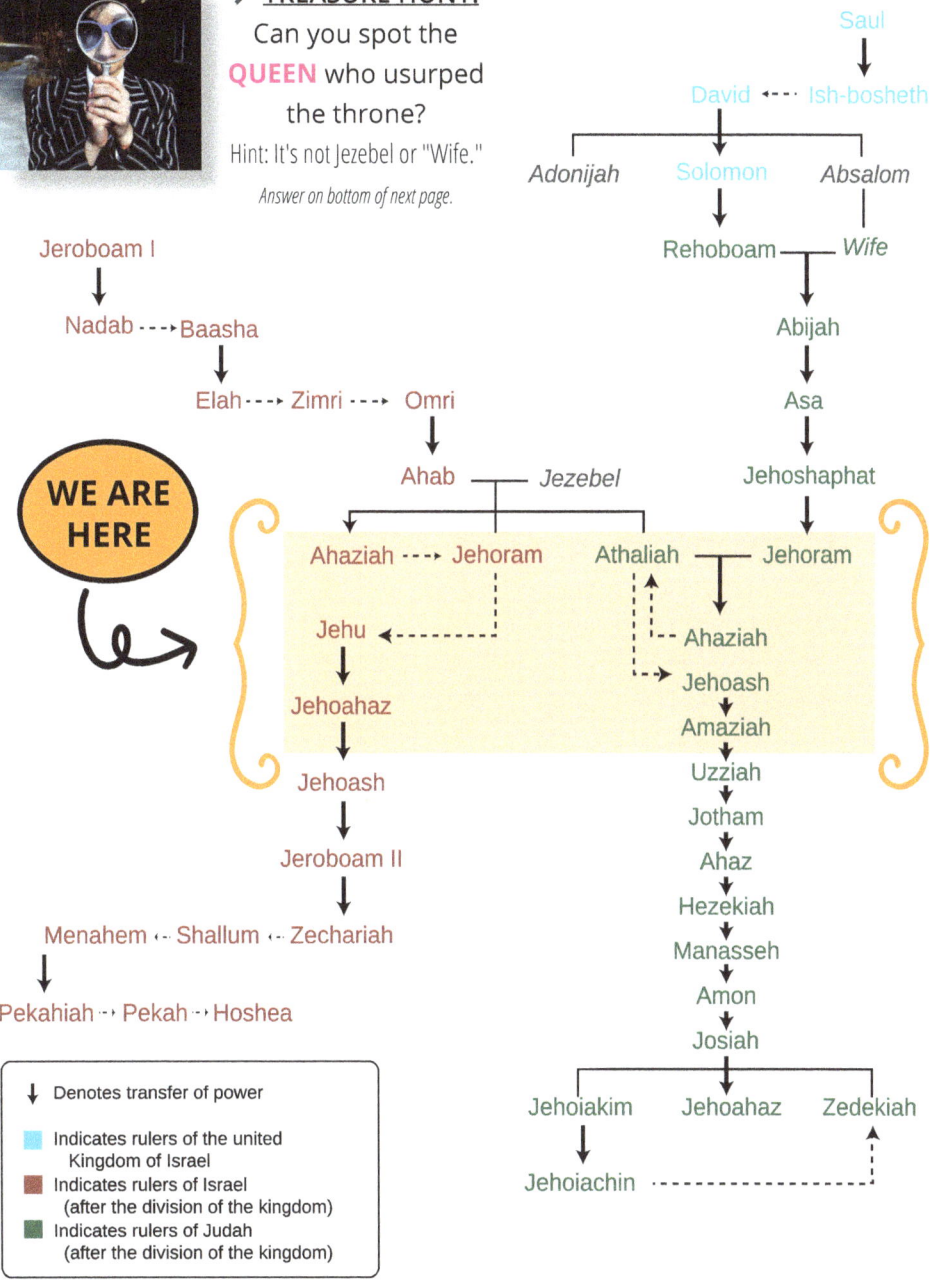

✎ **TREASURE HUNT:**

Can you spot the **QUEEN** who usurped the throne?

Hint: It's not Jezebel or "Wife."

Answer on bottom of next page.

Saul

David ◄--- Ish-bosheth

Adonijah Solomon Absalom

Jeroboam I

Nadab ---► Baasha

Rehoboam —— *Wife*

Abijah

Asa

Elah ---► Zimri ---► Omri

Jehoshaphat

Ahab —— *Jezebel*

WE ARE HERE

Ahaziah ---► Jehoram   Athaliah —— Jehoram

Jehu ◄------   Ahaziah

Jehoahaz   Jehoash

                  Amaziah

Jehoash   Uzziah

                  Jotham

Jeroboam II   Ahaz

                  Hezekiah

Menahem ◄-- Shallum ◄-- Zechariah   Manasseh

                  Amon

Pekahiah --► Pekah --► Hoshea   Josiah

Jehoiakim   Jehoahaz   Zedekiah

Jehoiachin -------------------

↓ Denotes transfer of power

■ Indicates rulers of the united Kingdom of Israel

■ Indicates rulers of Israel (after the division of the kingdom)

■ Indicates rulers of Judah (after the division of the kingdom)

As we learned in the previous chapter, Bathsheba eventually emerged as an influential presence in the palace. She strategically ensured that her son, Solomon, would inherit the throne by insisting David anoint him as co-regent before his death. When David died, Solomon was crowned King of Israel, solidified the Davidic Dynasty, and became famous in his own right. He was renowned for his wisdom, wealth, 700 wives 😄, and construction of the first Temple in Jerusalem: Solomon's Temple.

It's important to note that ONLY Saul, David, and Solomon reigned over a UNIFIED Israel. When Solomon died, his once unified kingdom split in two: the Northern Kingdom of Israel (10 tribes) and the Southern Kingdom of Judah (2 tribes). The capital of the Northern Kingdom was Samaria (a city), and the capital of the Southern Kingdom remained in Jerusalem where the Temple was located. Refer to the map on the following page to see how the tribes were organized into two kingdoms.

The leadership and spiritual direction of each kingdom often mirrored the actions and beliefs of its current royal family. When the kings followed the Lord, the people did, too. When they worshiped false gods like Baal, Molech, and Asherah, the people followed suit. Consequently, the spiritual state of the kingdoms fluctuated significantly from one monarch to the next.

One famous royal couple in the Northern Kingdom, King Ahab and Queen Jezebel, are remembered for their idolatry and luring people away from the Lord. Jezebel, in particular, is often singled out for her role in promoting the worship of Baal and Asherah (gods of her native Phoenician culture) and "killing off the prophets of the LORD" (1 Kings 18:4). You might recall the epic face-off where the prophets of Baal and the prophet Elijah engaged in a supernatural showdown on Mt. Carmel, testing whose deity truly reigned supreme. That would be Elijah's God: He brought the 🔥 🔥 🔥.

➡️ **Here is where we pick up our narrative for this chapter.**

At some point during the reign of Ahab and Jezebel in Israel, they likely enter into a peace treaty with King Jehoshaphat of Judah which is sealed by the marriage of their children. As reported by the famous first century Jewish historian, Flavius Josephus:

> Jehoshaphat took for his son Jehoram to [sic] wife the daughter of Ahab, the king of the ten tribes, whose name was Athaliah.[1]

This was a common custom among royal families in the ancient Near East who would use marriage as legally binding contracts to solidify peace treaties.

Did you catch that? It's an important detail so let's review it for clarity:

 JEHORAM, a prince of Judah (*Southern Kingdom*) marries
ATHALIAH, a princess of Israel (*Northern Kingdom*).

This strategic connection between the royal families cannot be overemphasized. Although she was not Jehoram's only wife, Athaliah becomes "Queen Mother" when their son inherits the throne 20+ years later.

THE DIVIDED KINGDOM

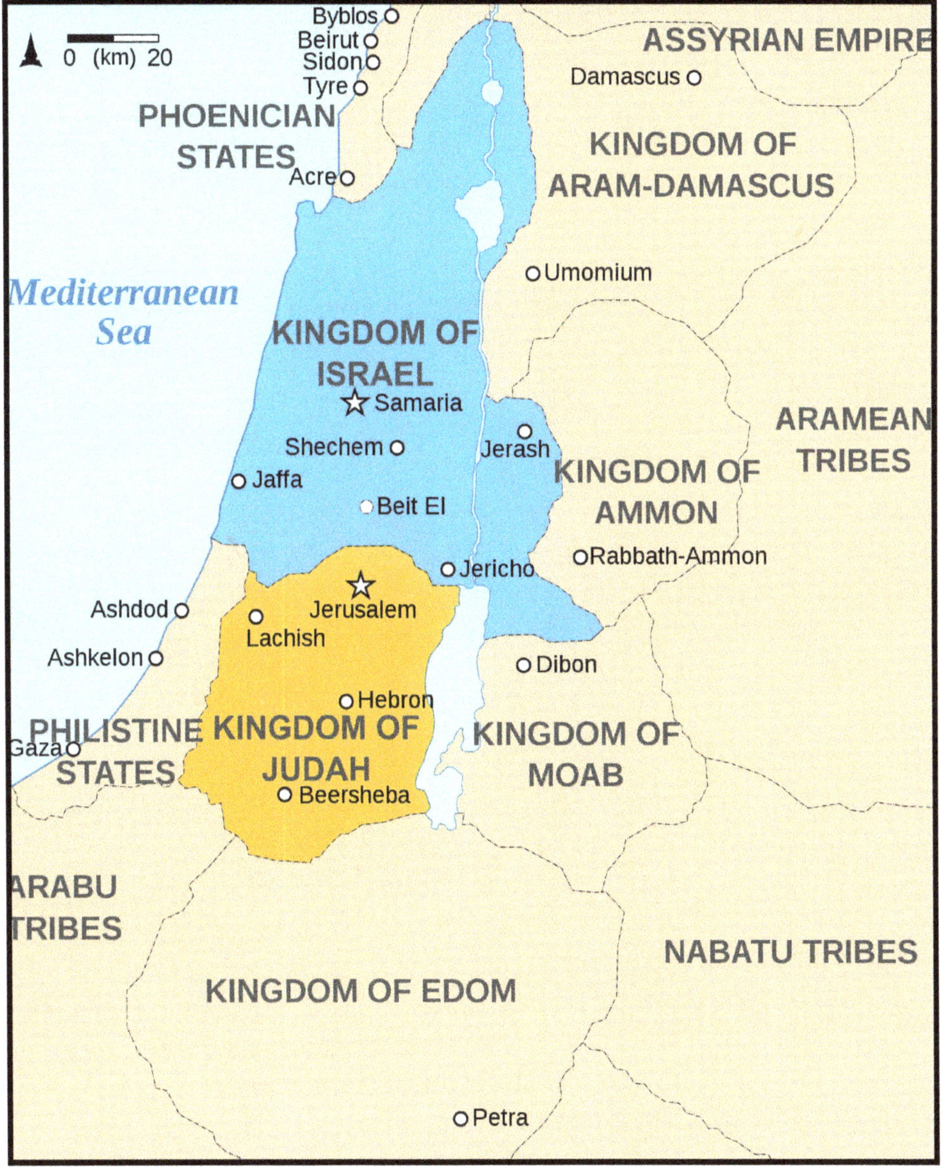

Map of the Divided Kingdom showing:

0 (km) 20

Byblos
Beirut
Sidon
Tyre
PHOENICIAN STATES
Acre

ASSYRIAN EMPIRE
Damascus

KINGDOM OF ARAM-DAMASCUS

Mediterranean Sea

Umomium

KINGDOM OF ISRAEL
☆ Samaria
Shechem
Jaffa
Beit El

Jerash

KINGDOM OF AMMON
Rabbath-Ammon

ARAMEAN TRIBES

Jericho

Ashdod
Ashkelon
☆ Jerusalem
Lachish
Hebron

Dibon

PHILISTINE STATES
Gaza

KINGDOM OF JUDAH
Beersheba

KINGDOM OF MOAB

ARABU TRIBES

NABATU TRIBES

KINGDOM OF EDOM

Petra

Athaliah's son, Ahaziah, is only 22 years old when he ascends the throne[2], and he is **heavily influenced** by his mother who still worships the gods of her deceased parents, Ahab and Jezebel. Together, mother and son promote Baal worship, and the young king does "what was evil in the sight of the LORD" (2 Chronicles 22:3-4). He reigns for **only one year**, until he is killed due to a series of unfortunate events.

Under normal circumstances, the crown of Judah would pass to the next direct descendant in the line of David; however, the succession process takes an unexpected and gruesome turn which surprises everyone. 😱

ATHALIAH'S RUTHLESS AMBITION

When news of her son's death reaches Athaliah, the Queen Mother, she takes matters into her own hands and **seize the throne for herself**. In a ruthless bid to consolidate power, Athaliah orders the **execution** of all potential royal heirs:

Side Note:
Queen Athaliah is the only woman to have reigned as a monarch in Israel/Judah; she reigned for six years from 842 BCE – 836 BCE.

Now when Athaliah, Ahaziah's mother, saw that her son was dead, she set about to destroy all the royal family of the house of Judah.
2 Chronicles 22:10

The historian Josephus further explains that Queen Athaliah's singular purpose in killing so many people is to ensure that no descendant of David's line could reclaim the throne. Ever. He writes:

She endeavored that NONE of the house of David might be left alive, but that the WHOLE FAMILY might be exterminated, that NO KING might arise out of it afterward.[3] (emphasis mine)

The Queen's evil scheme would have succeeded were it not for the **quick thinking** and **brave actions** of one of her stepdaughters: Jehosheba.[4]

AUNTIE JEHOSHEBA TO THE RESCUE!

As recorded in 2 Chronicles 22:11, Jehosheba is the sister of Athaliah's deceased son—they had the same father, but different mothers. Jehosheba is married to the high priest in Jerusalem so it's no surprise her actions are closely connected with Solomon's Temple.

When Jehosheba realizes that Queen Athaliah is killing everyone in line to the throne, **she immediately takes action.**

It's at this point in the narrative we learn that her late brother had a one-year-old son—and she's not about to let her baby nephew be murdered by her evil stepmother!

Jehosheba sneaks into the palace and stealthily rescues little Joash and his nurse. Quickly and quietly extracting them from the palace, Jehosheba stashes the baby and his nurse at the Temple where they remain in hiding for **SIX YEARS.** It's here that she and her husband, the high priest, raise the rightful heir to the throne, and you can bet they bring him up in the ways of the LORD.

There are a lot of theories about how Queen Athaliah could have neglected to murder the most obvious heir to the throne, but since her orders were carried out by her loyal followers and supporters, it's easy to imagine that those who *opposed* her lied and pretended the baby was dead.

 # A WOMAN ON JUDAH'S THRONE

Queen Athaliah seizes the throne and reigns in the Southern Kingdom of Judah *unchallenged* for six years—all the while oblivious that the rightful heir to the throne escaped her brutal massacre and is thriving nearby.

SOMETHING TO THINK ABOUT...

Jehosheba's story is about so much more than palace drama or family loyalty. Her swift and decisive actions played a pivotal role in preserving the lineage from which the Messiah was later prophesied to come, as recorded in scriptures such as Isaiah 11:1 and Jeremiah 23:5. **Her intervention ensured the survival of the Davidic line,** crucial for the fulfillment of the messianic promise held dear by future generations.

SIX YEARS LATER...

In a meticulously orchestrated, top secret, and invitation-only private ceremony, Jehosheba's husband, the high priest, anoints his 7-year-old nephew Joash as the rightful King of Judah, thereby returning the throne to the line of David.

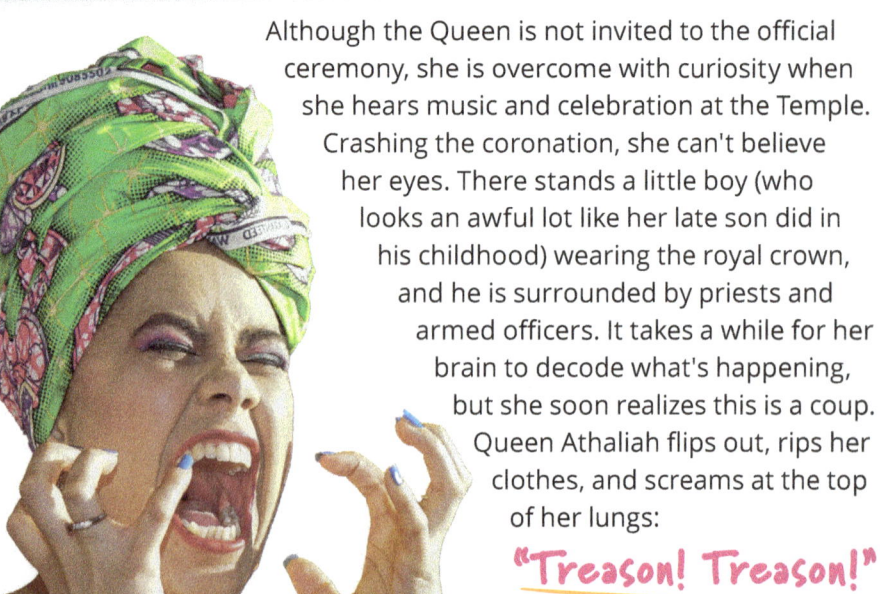

Although the Queen is not invited to the official ceremony, she is overcome with curiosity when she hears music and celebration at the Temple. Crashing the coronation, she can't believe her eyes. There stands a little boy (who looks an awful lot like her late son did in his childhood) wearing the royal crown, and he is surrounded by priests and armed officers. It takes a while for her brain to decode what's happening, but she soon realizes this is a coup. Queen Athaliah flips out, rips her clothes, and screams at the top of her lungs:

"Treason! Treason!"

Not surprisingly, the queen's cries are quickly silenced. Queen Athaliah flees the Temple through the horse gate, with troops in hot pursuit. In an ironic twist of fate, she is killed in the palace just as a direct descendant of David is being celebrated as the new King of Judah.

SEVEN YEARS OLD

Little Joash becomes king at the tender age of seven. Since the number seven symbolizes completion and perfection in the Bible, it's no coincidence that the family waits until he is seven years old to publicly anoint him and place the crown on his head. The timing underscores the notion that his ascension to the throne is a **God-ordained event**, ushering in a new chapter for Judah and a return to the worship of the LORD—at least for a time.

Joash's aunt Jehosheba and uncle, the high priest, each play a crucial role in his protection and eventual enthronement. They carefully orchestrate the coup against Queen Athaliah, ensuring the safety of Joash and the restoration of the Davidic line to the throne of Judah. Joash goes on to reign for 40 years.

In conclusion, when Jehosheba rescues baby Joash from Queen Athaliah's massacre of the royal heirs, she not only saves a life but single-handedly preserves the Davidic line. This is significant on another level because it is from David's descendants that the Messiah is later prophesied to emerge, as proclaimed by prophets such as Isaiah, Jeremiah, Ezekiel, and Micah.

And that's a *really* big deal!

"The days are surely coming," says the Lord,
"when I will raise up for David a righteous Branch,
and he shall reign as king and deal wisely and shall
execute justice and righteousness in the land.
In his days Judah will be saved, and Israel will live in safety.
And this is the name by which he will be called:
'The Lord is our righteousness.'"
Jeremiah 23:5-6

You can read about Jehosheba in **2 Kings 8-11** and **2 Chronicles 21-23**. 🌿

Personal Reflections

What stood out to you?

Did reading this chapter prompt further questions?

Look at the cover photo for this chapter and imagine why it was chosen. What do you notice?

Is there a woman in your life who, like **Jehosheba**, discovered something bad was happening and took immediate action to protect another? Someone who stopped a rumor from spreading, thus protecting another's reputation? Or someone who did what was necessary to remove a child (or anyone!) from an abusive situation?

Consider sending her a quick text, encouraging message, or longer letter to let her know you're thinking of her today. Acknowledge her discernment, bravery, and compassion, and/or share how she inspires your walk with God.

If the woman you thought of is you, please send a message to the author at: info@valiantwomenofthebible.com so we can bear witness to your story.

 ## INTRODUCING: THE SAMARITANS

After Assyria conquered the Northern Kingdom of Israel in 722 BCE, they executed their usual strategy of mass deportations and resettling conquered peoples. This diverse mix of refugees created a tremendous dependence on the Assyrian Empire (which was the goal) and set the stage for cultural and religious fusion. Interactions among the resettled groups and the remnant of native Israelites in the capital city of Samaria led to the fusion of diverse traditions and intermarriage, resulting in a new people group known as the "Samaritans." When the first wave of Jewish exiles returned from Babylon in 538 BCE, they discovered the remnant population had intermarried with the foreigners. This ethnic blending was later condemned by Ezra when he arrived back in Jerusalem with a second wave of exiles around 458 BCE, contributing to long-standing tensions between the Jews and Samaritans.

Samaria, former capital of the Northern Kingdom. Today an archaeological site.

Huldah

PROPHET TEACHER

"She declared to them,
'Thus says the Lord, the God of Israel...'"
2 Chronicles 34:23

Huldah

We first meet Huldah at her home in Jerusalem; she is married to the "keeper of the king's wardrobe" and might be working on a lesson for her students.

Jewish tradition holds that "Huldah had a school for women in Jerusalem, whom she taught the word of G-d insofar as it pertained to Jewish women, mothers and daughters."[1] While some believe Huldah teaches in public, others suggest she is a teacher only to women. *This is tradition, not in the Scripture.* What we know for sure is she's a **prophet**.

 ## HISTORICAL SETTING

The events in this chapter take place approximately **215 years after the coronation of King Joash** (*see previous chapter*). One of the initiatives established during Joash's 40-year reign plays a **direct role** in Huldah's story. I find that connection absolutely fascinating!

After King Joash died, significant changes occurred in the Holy Land, two of which directly impact the historical setting for this story: (1) the obliteration of the Northern Kingdom of Israel, and (2) the dilapidation of Solomon's Temple.

Firstly, the Northern Kingdom of Israel no longer exists. **Israel was destroyed in 722 BCE** when the Assyrians invaded and forcibly relocated its inhabitants by dispersing them all over their massive empire. 20 years later, they attacked Judah causing significant damage. They captured several key cities, but they did not conquer Judah in the same way they did Israel. Secondly, Solomon's Temple in Jerusalem is in a state of disrepair due to **decades** of abuse and neglect.

The current King of Judah is named Josiah, and he worships the LORD; however, his father and grandfather did not. During his grandfather's 55 year reign, he built altars to false gods INSIDE the Temple! He also practiced witchcraft and sorcery and even sacrificed one of his own sons in the fire to the false god Molech. When he died, his son (Josiah's dad) took over and carried on his father's practices until his murder two years later. Both men turned people **away** from God. But then, Josiah inherits the throne.

Similar to King Joash who was anointed king at the ripe old age of seven, Josiah is crowned King at a whopping eight years old. And that's not all they have in common: They also share a deep-seeded appreciation for Solomon's Temple.

Confronted with the spiritually destructive legacies of his grandfather and father, the young King Josiah determines early on to ditch the family tradition of worshiping false gods and **FOLLOW GOD** with his whole heart. Josiah is remembered for his spiritual reforms and his dedication to the Lord.

In his mid-twenties, King Josiah orders a major clean-up and renovation of the run-down Temple—even though it will cost an exorbitant amount of money. To fund this project, King Josiah sends his secretary to the high priest with orders to **add up all the silver that's been collected at the threshold of the Temple** over the years for Temple maintenance (2 Kings 22:3-7).

And guess who set-up that fund? 200+ years earlier, when Joash reigned as the King of Judah, he instituted a **special offering for the upkeep of the Temple**. He was likely influenced by his Aunt Jehosheba and Uncle Jehoiada, the High Priest, who raised him. Thanks to their long-term planning, King Josiah will use this collection to restore the Temple and pay the carpenters, builders, masons, and any other workers they might need to hire.

THE *REAL* TEMPLE TREASURE

Following King Josiah's instructions, the high priest heads to the Temple to tally the donations. It's during this silver-counting expedition he discovers a treasure **way more valuable than silver**: "the Book of the Law."

The fact that the high priest "discovers" this scroll underscores its sad condition: It's been neglected and forgotten for decades—which makes sense in light of what we know was going on during the reigns of King Josiah's father and grandfather and prior rulers in Judah.

When the high priest shares this sacred "treasure" with the king's secretary, he receives the scroll and immediately takes it to the king.

Side Note:
The "Book of the Law" mentioned in the biblical text isn't a paperback or hardback book like what we're used to reading nowadays, it was a scroll. While we can't be certain of the exact passages it included, many scholars believe it was the book of *Deuteronomy*, or at least a significant portion of it. This is supported by the type of national religious reforms initiated by King Josiah after its discovery. These reforms, based on the covenant principles outlined in *Deuteronomy*, included: (1) the centralization of worship in Jerusalem; (2) the destruction of idolatrous shrines; and (3) a Passover celebration strictly adhering to the stipulations recorded in *Deuteronomy*.

Upon his arrival, King Josiah has his secretary read the scroll aloud to him, and he listens intently to the words. Slowly, reality sinks in as he reflects on how far the nation has strayed from God's laws.

In a dramatic act of contrition, the king rips his robes and then orders the high priest, the court secretary, and two others to **verify the scroll's authenticity**—they need to know if the scroll is, indeed, what they think it is:

> Go and inquire of the LORD for me, the people, and all Judah about the words in this book that has been found.
> 2 Kings 22:13

This is a royal command to visit a trusted prophet of the Lord—and their choice of prophet might surprise you.

Photo of a Dead Sea Scroll featuring a section of Deuteronomy *with the Ten Commandments*

A PROPHET NAMED HULDAH

When King Josiah's most trusted envoys leave the palace to "inquire of the LORD," they choose not to seek out the prophet Jeremiah or the prophet Zephaniah—even though they were both prophesying in the Jerusalem area at that time.

Instead, the group of men head straight for the second district in Jerusalem to the home of a prophet named Huldah. As Edith Deen keenly observes in *All the Women of the Bible*:

> *Evidently Huldah was known in the kingdom of Judah far and wide or she would never have been sought out by King Josiah...He had faith in Huldah's spiritual powers, and he wanted her to tell him whether the book was genuine or not.[2]*

Their choice to consult Huldah—despite their proximity to male prophets—speaks volumes about her respected status and their faith in her ability to inquire of the Lord and receive spiritual insight.

It's clear that Huldah's sex does not preclude her from exercising her spiritual gift in the presence of men. The fact that the high priest was part of the delegation underscores this important point.

Just let that sink in for a moment.

Side Note:
The Dead Sea Scrolls were discovered in 1947 and instantly provided us with some of the oldest manuscripts of the Hebrew Bible available.

Once informed about the Temple restoration and the king's inquiry regarding the 'Book of the Law,' Huldah carefully examines the scroll and takes some time to seek guidance from the Lord. As a prophet, it's important that she not jump to conclusions or insert her personal opinions into the message.

Since prophets are often called by God to deliver tough truths to powerful people, they must be certain of the Source of the message and have the courage to speak it aloud, regardless of the consequences. It's risky delivering a message that those in power don't want to hear.

Huldah is someone who truly lives up to this challenge, with both the confidence to trust what God has revealed to her and the courage to speak it out loud, with no concern for her own safety.

A WORD FROM THE LORD

Having received a word from the Lord, Huldah delivers the message to the king's envoys. Her approach mirrors that of other prophets like Isaiah, Jeremiah, and Ezekiel, emphasizing her role as merely the messenger.

- ❖ "Thus says the LORD, the God of Israel..." (2 Kings 22:15)
- ❖ "Thus says the LORD..." (2 Kings 22: 16)
- ❖ "Thus says the LORD, the God of Israel..." (2 Kings 22:18)
- ❖ "I also have heard you, says the LORD. Therefore, I will..." (2 Kings 22:19-20)

Making it clear that she is speaking **only** what she has heard, faithfully transmitting God's words without addition or alteration, Huldah boldly utters **FOUR** prophetic statements:

1. **Disaster for Jerusalem and Its Inhabitants**—By turning their backs on God and worshiping other gods, they have provoked the Lord's anger.

2. **Consequences of Idolatry**—The disaster is directly tied to their actions. God's wrath has been kindled against Jerusalem: It will not be quenched.

3. **A Personal Message to King Josiah**—Because of his sincere surprise and authentic repentance before the Lord, Josiah's cries have been heard by God.

4. **A Promise of a Proper Burial for King Josiah**—Despite the impending disaster for his kingdom, King Josiah is promised that when he dies, he will have a proper burial, and he will be spared from witnessing the destruction of Jerusalem.

A NOTABLE CONTRIBUTION

During her response to the king's envoys, **Huldah does something that no other prophet has ever done before: She bases her pronouncements on the words _written_ in the Book of the Law**, and this action serves to authenticate its genuineness and validate its authority.

This is huge, and God uses a WOMAN to do it.

As Claudia V. Camp points out in her article "Huldah: Bible" in *The Shalvi/ Hyman Encyclopedia of Jewish Women*:

"Her validation of a text thus stands as the first recognizable act in the long process of canon formation. Huldah authenticates a document as being GOD'S WORD, thereby affording it the sanctity required for establishing a text as authoritative, or canonical."

Side Note:
Canon with one "n" is not a typo. It's a word used to describe the collection of sacred scriptures gathered into the Bible. It's a boundary word, because canonization is a systematic process by which texts are **recognized as authoritative and inspired and, therefore, included in the Bible** and which ones are rejected and excluded.

👑 MEANWHILE, BACK AT THE PALACE

When the envoys return to the palace and relay Huldah's pronouncements, King Josiah gets right to work. First, he calls together all the elders, priests, and prophets from throughout Judah, as well as everyone living in Jerusalem and the surrounding area. Once everyone has gathered, they head up to the Temple (currently under renovation). In the outer court, King Josiah himself reveals the discovery of the "Book of the Law" and reads it aloud to the crowd. Then, he takes a significant step towards restoring the nation's right relationship with God by doing something that hasn't been done in Judah in a really, really long time: He makes a new covenant with the Lord.

> The king stood by the pillar and made a covenant before the LORD,
> to follow the LORD, keeping his commandments, his decrees,
> and his statutes, with all his heart and all his soul, to perform
> the words of this covenant that were written in this book.
> ALL THE PEOPLE joined in the covenant.
> 2 Kings 23:3 (emphasis mine)

King Josiah dedicates himself to leading a **NATIONWIDE SPIRITUAL CLEANSE**. To enact these sweeping reforms, the priests are empowered to:

- Remove idols and unholy vessels from *inside* Solomon's Temple and burn them *outside* the city. 🔥
- Tear down the "high places" dedicated to Baal and Asherah worship anywhere in Judah and depose their priests.
- Purify the Temple and commit everything they do to the Lord.

Do you think King Josiah would have undertaken this these massive reforms had Huldah sugar-coated or softened the clear message from the Lord?

CONCLUSION

Despite King Josiah's visionary leadership and his mighty efforts to turn the people's hearts back to God, each of Huldah's prophecies is fulfilled exactly as she said. Notably, **Huldah passes all the tests for a true prophet of the Lord.** (*See "Digging Deeper" on pages 132-133 for a list of qualifications.*)

Listed here are a handful of significant events which occur subsequently in the Southern Kingdom of Judah:

- Within 40 years of Huldah's prophecies, King Josiah dies and is buried;
- Two years later, Judah is invaded by the Babylonians under King Nebuchadnezzar, and Solomon's Temple is looted and destroyed;
- Many of Jerusalem's most prominent families and youth (including Daniel, Shadrach, Meshach, and Abednego) are forcibly relocated to Babylon—along with the Temple treasure. This is called the **Babylonian Exile** which lasts approximately 70 years.

You can see the Prophet Huldah in action in **2 Kings 22** and **2 Chronicles 34**. ✎

Personal Reflections

What stood out to you?

Did reading this chapter prompt further questions?

Look at the cover photo for this chapter and imagine why it was chosen. What do you notice?

Is there a woman in your life who, like **Huldah**, seems to have a direct channel to the Lord? Someone who has been called upon to speak truth to power regardless of personal consequences? Someone who is respected by her peers and known for her spiritual discernment?

Consider sending her a quick text, encouraging message, or longer letter to let her know you're thinking of her today. Acknowledge her gifting, wisdom, and courage, and/or share how she inspires your walk with God.

If the woman you thought of is you, please send a message to the author at: **info@valiantwomenofthebible.com** so we can bear witness to your story. Been there.

SOAPBOX MOMENT

In a society obsessed with hierarchy, power, and status, we need to remember that God often works through people who clash with our expectations. This divine pattern of inclusion underscores the depth of His love for each of us, and far surpasses the restrictions some have placed on leadership and spiritual authority based on one's sex, marital status, or fashion sense.

God has NEVER limited Himself to speaking only through male voices. When the Lord chose Deborah and Huldah to be prophets, He demonstrated that the power to influence and shape the course of faith communities is accessible to whomever He calls.[3]

Huldah's story is an invitation for us to widen our perspectives and embrace a more diverse and inclusive view of spiritual leadership.

DIGGING DEEPER

Scattered throughout Scripture are specific criteria we can use as a kind of "litmus test" to determine whether or not someone is a true prophet of God. These are not based on logical fallacies, such as the "No True Scotsman" argument, but on specific, defined attributes and character traits which are not arbitrary. These guidelines help us discern the authenticity of a prophet's claims and the authority behind their words so we know whom to trust *and* whom to disregard.

Here are five key qualifications of a prophet of God:

1 A PROPHET OF GOD WILL SPEAK IN ALIGNMENT WITH GOD'S WORD.

A true prophet's teachings must be consistent with the teachings and commandments of God as already revealed in Scripture. Anything contrary to what has already been revealed is a red flag (Isaiah 8:20).

2 PREDICTIONS MADE BY A PROPHET OF GOD WILL BE FULFILLED.

A true prophet's predictions will come to pass. *"If a prophet speaks in the name of the Lord but the thing does not take place or prove true, it is a word that the Lord has NOT SPOKEN. The prophet has spoken it presumptuously, do not be frightened by it"* Deuteronomy 18:22. In other words, if a prophet's prediction fails, they did not hear it from God. Therefore, be on guard.

3 A PROPHET OF GOD WILL PROMOTE WORSHIP OF THE LORD.

A true prophet must lead people toward worshiping the LORD and not toward other gods. Scripture warns against prophets or "dreamers of dreams" who try to turn people away from God, even if some of their signs and wonders come true (Deuteronomy 13:1-4).

A PROPHET OF GOD WILL EXHIBIT MORAL INTEGRITY AND RIGHTEOUSNESS.

Scripture consistently shows that the character and actions of a true prophet will reflect God's attributes of righteousness, justice, and compassion (Jeremiah 22:3). Prophets are expected to embody and advocate for fairness, to defend the oppressed, and to act with integrity (Isaiah 1:17). Their lives and messages should align with God's commands to seek justice, show mercy, and walk humbly with Him (Micah 6:8).

A PROPHET OF GOD WILL BE RECOGNIZED AS SUCH BY THE PEOPLE OF GOD.

In many instances, true prophets are accepted and affirmed by godly people in their local community. This is not a standalone sign, since sometimes hindsight is 20/20, as was the case for the prophet Jeremiah. Often, though, local support can indicate confirmation of a prophet's calling. We see this principle in action when Huldah is sought out as a trusted local prophet—a woman who could reliably inquire of and hear from the LORD. Her prophetic gift is recognized by the high priest and the king.

This list outlines the essential qualifications for a true prophet of God, and these criteria remain just as valid today as they were in biblical times. When we encounter individuals claiming prophetic authority, it's crucial to remain vigilant and steadfast in evaluating their words. Remember, a true prophet's life, message, and counsel will reflect God's character, marked by integrity, compassion, and humility.

Therefore, if a prophet advocates for supporting a leader who lacks these key moral attributes, they are directly contradicting biblical principles and they are not speaking for God.

It is OUR responsibility to carefully vet the sources of information we consume. We do this by rooting ourselves in the Word, practicing spiritual discernment through prayer and fasting, and evaluating prophets according to these guidelines. Additionally, we must stay humble and open to receiving new information from diverse sources. In this way, we protect ourselves against idolatry, ensuring our beliefs and actions are aligned with a sincere pursuit of truth and God's will for our lives.

SIMPLE TIMELINE OF ISRAEL'S HISTORY
500 BCE – 37 BCE

This timeline includes some of the most significant events and notable figures from the Second Temple Period.

486 BCE - 465 BCE
- Reign of Ahasuerus (Xerxes I of Persia), during which the events of the book of *Esther* are set.

458-445 BCE
- Ezra the Scribe leads a second wave of exiles back to Jerusalem and enforces the Law.
- Nehemiah returns to Jerusalem to rebuild walls.

432 BCE
- Malachi, the last prophet of the Hebrew Bible, delivers his prophecies.

332 BCE
- Conquest of the region by Alexander the Great.
- End of Persian rule; Start of Hellenistic period.

323 BCE
- Death of Alexander the Great.
- His empire is divided amongst his four generals, establishing several Hellenistic kingdoms.

320 BCE
- General Ptolemy I takes control of Egypt and also exerts control over Judea.*

312 BCE
- General Seleucus I Nicator establishes the Seleucid Empire, including Syria and later Judea.

301 BCE
- Battle of Ipsus: The Seleucid and Ptolemaic kingdoms solidify their divisions after the defeat of General Antigonus I Monophthalmus.

200 - 198 BCE
- Antiochus III the Great of the Seleucid Empire conquers Judea.
- The Battle of Panium: Seleucid victory further secures their control over Judea.

175 BCE
- Antiochus IV Epiphanes becomes the Seleucid king & intensifies Hellenization efforts in Judea.

168 BCE
- Antiochus IV Epiphanes desecrates the Second Temple, inciting a major Jewish revolt.

167 BCE - 160 BCE
- The Maccabbean Revolt: Led by the priest Judas Maccabeus and his brothers against Seleucid rule, resulting in 100 years of autonomy.

164 BCE
- The Maccabees rededicate the Second Temple
- Hanukkah established to celebrate the miracle of one day's oil lasting for eight days.

152 BCE
- Jonathan Apphus becomes High Priest, and consolidates religious and political power in Jerusalem. He is pivotal in establishing the Hasmoneans as rulers over Judea. "Hasmonean" indicates the ancestral family name.

140 BCE
- Simon Thassi, another brother, takes control and becomes the first to be recognized as prince and High Priest of the Hasmonean dynasty.

63 BCE
- Rome conquers Judea, establishing control under Pompey the Great.

37 BCE
- Herod the Great marries a Hasmonean princess and is crowned "King" of Judea under Rome.
- Herod transforms Judea's landscape with many architectural projects, notably the massive expansion and renovation of the Second Temple.

* During the Hellenistic period, the territory of **Judah was renamed to Judea**. This renaming reflects the broader Hellenization of the region, which involved the introduction of Greek culture, language, and administrative practices by the new Macedonian rulers. This marked a significant transformation in the Judean cultural and political landscape.

chapter sixteen

Vashti

NON-COMPLIANT QUEEN

"But Queen Vashti refused to
come at the king's command
conveyed by the eunuchs."
Esther 1:12a

Vashti

When we first meet Vashti, we learn that she is the married to King Ahasuerus. The exact identification of Ahasuerus is debated among scholars, but most identify him as Xerxes I,
a theory widely accepted in both Jewish and Christian tradition.

To be precise, Vashti is the Queen of the Persian Empire in what is now modern-day Iran.

Crown of the Empress of Iran ca. 1967

 ## HISTORICAL SETTING

Our story begins in the third year of King Ahasuerus' reign in 482 BCE at the end of a 180-day royal exhibition at his palace in Susa (Persia's capital city). For six months, he has entertained his officials, ministers, armies, nobles and governors showing off "the vast wealth of his kingdom and glory of his majesty" with lots of pomp and circumstance (Esther 1:3-4).

King Ahasuerus hosts his long exhibition in the **Palace of Darius** which was built by his father Darius I at Susa. *Pictured above.*

Side Note:
Susa (also called "Shushan") was one of four capitals of the Persian Empire during King Ahasuerus' reign. Located in modern day Iran, Susa has been declared a World Heritage Site by UNESCO. You can view more photos of Ancient Susa and the artifacts discovered there on the UNESCO website at https://whc.unesco.org.

AND NOW, BACK TO THE PAR-TAY!

After spending half a year hosting elite-only celebrations, the royal couple is hosting a week-long banquet to wrap things up, and **EVERYONE** in Susa is invited—from the least to the greatest. And the royal wine is flowing freely.

▶▶ **Fast forward to day seven:** Vashti is busy hosting a royal banquet for the **women** of the kingdom **inside** the palace while her husband is hosting a separate banquet for the **men** *outside* in the palace garden, as it was customary for Persian men and women to dine separately at public feasts.

Human-Headed Aladlammu Sormounted by the Winged Sun of Ahura Mazda
Apadana Palace of Darius I in Susa

On the final day of the feast, the king realizes this is his last chance to make a big impression on his subjects. Therefore, in one final show of his great authority, power, and majesty, the king commands **seven** of his eunuchs to bring him Queen Vashti—wearing her crown—so he could show off her beauty to all in attendance. That is, all the men in attendance. Remember, EVERYONE is at the party *from the least to the greatest*.

When the queen receives the king's command,

SHE **REFUSES** TO OBEY.

Just let that sink in: It's a pretty big deal to refuse the King of Persia, no matter who you are—but it's an especially big deal when you're his wife.

WHAT DID HE _REALLY_ WANT?

Although the **Hebrew scripture is silent** about Vashti's reasons for rejecting the king's request, the _Targum Sheni_ to _Esther_ elaborates on the story, adding a salacious detail: the king instructs seven eunuchs to bring his wife to him wearing her crown—ONLY her crown.[1] (_See Side Note._)

Regardless of his specific instructions and in spite of being summoned by seven eunuchs, Queen Vashti has zero desire to be humiliated in front of a crowd of drunken men. She refuses to be a character in the king's ridiculous exhibition.

The writers at the Women's League for Conservative Judaism offer the following insight:

Side Note:
The Targums are Aramaic translations and interpretations of the Hebrew Scriptures. They were developed over many centuries to provide explanations and expansions of the original text in the language of the people (Jesus and his disciples spoke Aramaic). While they incorporate elements of oral tradition, they also reflect the interpretive traditions and cultural contexts of the Jewish communities who produced them.

> Vashti may be the first recorded woman to "JUST SAY NO." From today's vantage point, we can only guess that she was so empowered because of the presence and support of the other women at HER banquet.[2] (emphasis mine)

There's nothing quite like a group of women to support, encourage, and empower each other to be brave and do hard things—especially when it involves standing up for themselves and preserving their dignity.

FRIEZE OF GRIFFINS
ca. 510 BCE
Originally discovered at
Apadana, West Courtyard
Palace of Darius I
Susa, Iran

Currently on display at
The Louvre Museum
Paris, France

TALK TO THE HAND ✋

The Queen risks it all by refusing to appear on demand, infuriating the king. In response, King Ahasuerus consults his seven closest advisors who agree that Vashti's behavior is inexcusable. As Sidnie White Crawford keenly observes in her commentary on *Esther* in the *Women's Bible Commentary*:

> The author here introduces a touch of the burlesque;
> Vashti's refusal to comply with the king's demand is perceived
> by the men as a grave threat to the dominance of every husband
> in the kingdom. Ahasuerus and his courtiers appear as
> hapless buffoons before the calm strength of Vashti,
> and by implication, of all their wives![3]

Vashti's refusal to come when the king summoned her was equivalent to breaking the law. This perfectly contrasts with her successor's decision to break the law when she appears before the king *without* an official summons. We'll cover her story in the next chapter.

"NO CROWN FOR YOU!"

In a **highly public** and **intentionally humiliating** punishment for this act of insubordination, King Ahasuerus strips Vashti of her crown and title, and then **permanently bans her** from his presence.

The king makes an example of Vashti, hoping to send a clear message to all wives and future wives throughout the Persian Empire: Disrespect your husband, and you will be severely punished.* Of course, we'll never really know if the womenfolk got the memo. 😉

One positive outcome for Vashti is that she gets what she wants: She never has to appear on demand before the king ever again. Isn't it ironic?

You can read the story about Vashti in **Esther 1**. ✺

Please Note: Vashti's story should never be interpreted as a mandate for women to obey their husbands. That interpretation completely misses the point. Instead, this part of the story spotlights the incredible courage it takes for a woman to stand up for herself and defend her dignity, even at great personal cost. This act of bravery, also echoed by Esther later in the story, teaches us that there are times when we must stand up for what is right, regardless of the consequences. And it reassures us that, indeed, we can do hard things.

Personal Reflections

What stood out to you?

Did reading this chapter prompt further questions?

Look at the cover photo for this chapter and imagine why it was chosen. What do you notice?

Is there a woman in your life who, like **Vashti**, demonstrates unwavering courage and personal integrity? Someone whose actions speak volumes about self-worth, even in the face of adversity? Have you witnessed her fearlessly standing up for what is right, regardless of personal consequences?

Consider sending her a quick text, encouraging message, or longer letter to let her know you're thinking of her today. Acknowledge her bravery and courage and share how she inspires you to navigate your own challenges with authenticity and conviction, and/or share how she inspires your walk with God.

If the woman you thought of is you, please send a message to the author at: <u>info@valiantwomenofthebible.com</u> so we can bear witness to your story.

Frieze of Four Melophores
(Immortal Persian Guard)
ca. 510 BCE

Originally discovered at Apadana Palace of Darius I in Susa on display at the Louvre.

chapter seventeen

Hadassah Esther

PEOPLE PROTECTOR

"I will go to the king, though it is against the law,
and if I perish, I perish."
Esther 4:16b

Hadassah
Esther

When we first meet Hadassah (Hebrew for "myrtle tree") she is living with her cousin Mordecai. Hadassah's parents died when she was very young, so her cousin Mordecai adopted her and raised her as his own daughter. The two of them live in the citadel of Susa, one of the four capital cities of the Persian Empire. Hadassah's story is directly set up by, and deeply intertwined with, the public humiliation and removal of Queen Vashti from her royal position. (*See previous chapter.*)

 ## HISTORICAL SETTING

As we learned in the chapter on Huldah, thousands of Jewish families were forcibly relocated to Babylon after Jerusalem fell to King Nebuchadnezzar. Decades later, the Persian Empire defeated and absorbed the Babylonian Empire under the leadership of Cyrus the Great.

In 537 BCE, Cyrus issued a decree permitting Jewish exiles to return to *Yehud* (Judah); he also offered to pay for the reconstruction of their Temple. Although some jumped at the chance to move back home, many did not. They had "bloomed where they were planted," having established new traditions and practicing their religion with no need of a brick-and-mortar Temple.

Hadassah's story is set more than a century after the original deportation of Jews to Babylon and 50 years after Cyrus' decree they could return home.

✳ **Mordecai and Hadassah are NOT exiles. They live in a flourishing Jewish community in Shushan (a.k.a. Susa)—enjoying life as Jews in the diaspora.** ✳

🌹 THE BACHELOR: "ROYAL EDITION"

When the king removes Queen Vashti from her royal position and bans her from coming into his presence ever again, he instantly becomes the most eligible bachelor in the Persian Empire. And it's not long until his servants come up with a plan to find him a new queen—they pitch him an idea for a new reality TV show: "The Bachelor: Royal Edition." 😉

The plot is simple, yet elegant: Producers would gather beautiful young virgins from all 127 provinces of the Empire, from India to Cush (Ethiopia/Sudan), and move them to the Darius Palace in Susa where they would live in a harem.

As part of harem life, the virgins would be trained in Persian royal etiquette and receive a total makeover. Then, each night, he would take a different virgin on a date for a chance to make a genuine love connection. 💕

The young woman would be treated like a queen during their spectacular evening together (remember, the king is an exhibitionist). At the end of the night, she would return to the harem, and he would make his way to the "Royal Diary Room" where he would go straight to camera and record his unfiltered thoughts about the evening and that particular date.

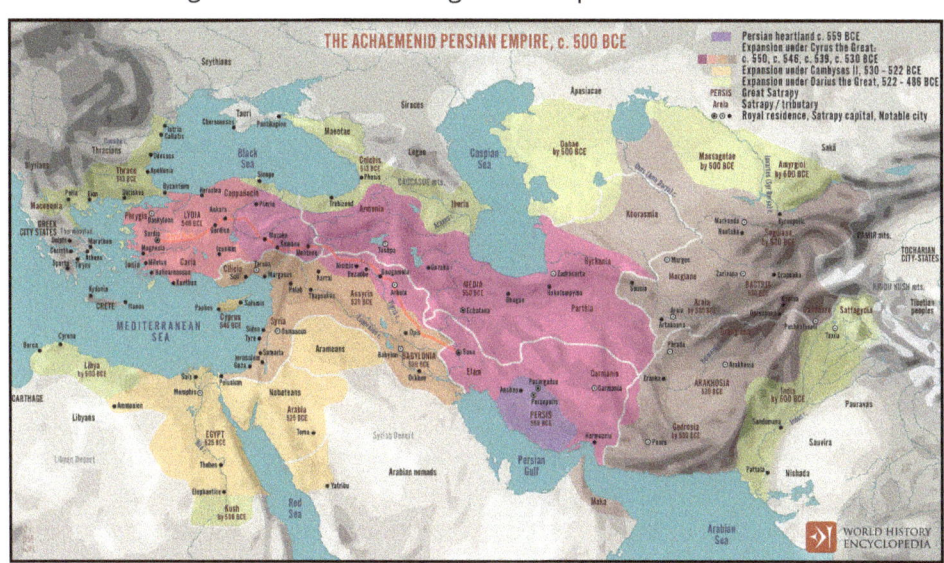

Map reprinted with permission of Simeon Netchev / World History Encyclopedia

King Ahasuerus (a.k.a. Xerxes the Great) ascended the throne when his father, Darius the Great, died in 486 BCE. At that time, "the Persian Empire stretched from Europe's Balkan Peninsula—in parts of what is present day Bulgaria, Romania and Ukraine—to the Indus River Valley in Northwest India and south to Egypt."[1] Xerxes himself is most remembered for his invasion of Greece and the battles of Thermopylae, Salamis, and Plataea which marked the beginning of the decline of the Achaemenid Empire.[2]

Once the king meets the young woman who captures his heart, he would present her with a beautiful, long-stemmed red rose, freshly cut from the royal gardens.

Later, during their live-streamed wedding ceremony, she would be crowned as the new "Queen of Persia." The ratings would be off the charts! 😆

REAL LIFE > REALITY TV

Okay, okay. The king's attendants don't actually pitch him on a show for *reality TV*; instead, they pitch him on a **REAL LIFE**, empire-wide "Queen Search."

It's the same overall plan but without all the modern technology. Instead of live cameras in every room, the virgins' activities would be observed and reported to him by the eunuchs. And he wouldn't be required to record any videos in the Royal Diary Room. The servants hold their breath waiting for his response. Thankfully, they don't have to wait long. The king is all in, on one condition: all he has to do is show up for the dates. 😉

Isn't it intriguing to see how much influence others have over the king's life? This is a consistent theme we see throughout the book of *Esther*. It appears that the king doesn't make any decisions on his own in the entire narrative.

HADASSAH IN THE HAREM

Side Note:
In the palace harem, Hadassah is not known by her Jewish name since she was advised by Mordecai to hide her ethnicity. Instead, she is known only by her Persian name: Esther, which means *star*. ✡️

Since Hadassah meets the queen-search criteria—pretty, virgin, breathing—she is collected and relocated to the harem along with way too many other young women from across the empire.

Do they speak the same language? Do they have any idea what's happening? Are they confused? Do they realize they will be in competition with each other for the position of queen? Do they know whom to trust?

As it turns out, the harem is managed by one of the king's most trusted eunuchs: Hegai. They oversee all the women in the house, and they notice Hadassah almost immediately. There's just *something* about her that intrigues them, and they take special interest in her. Hegai keeps an eye on Hadassah, now called Esther (*see Side Note on previous page*), and they ensure she receives preferential treatment. **Hegai shows Esther great favor.**

As the head eunuch, Hegai sets Esther up with "the best place in the harem" and provides her with a number of personal attendants. She is offered better food to eat than the other virgins; she receives regular beauty treatments; and when the time comes for Esther's special night with the king, Hegai makes sure she knows what to take with her in order to make the very best impression on Ahasuerus.

Predictably, the king falls hard for Esther and presents her with a metaphorical red rose. 🌹 😍 Soon, they are married, and there is much feasting in the land.

BUT THEN... PLOT TWIST! 🎭

In a completely unrelated series of events taking place outside the palace, Esther's cousin Mordecai disrespects one of the king's top-seated officials, Haman the Agagite. Mordecai refuses to bow to him, even though the king has commanded it. When his friends inquire why he disregards the king's edict, Mordecai reminds them he is Jewish and will never bow to the Agagite.

Drastically overreacting, Haman decides to destroy Mordecai and everyone like him: His deepest desire is to kill **ALL** the Jewish people in Persia, and he'll do whatever it takes to make it happen. As a sycophant, Haman strokes the king's ego, shares vague news of an imminent threat, offers to handle it himself, and secures the authority he needs to annihilate the Jews. It's clear, at this point, King Ahasuerus is oblivious to the chaos and instability an edict like this will create throughout the empire—but he is alone in his ignorance. Everyone else gets it. And when the queen's cousin, Mordecai, hears of Haman's evil plans, he turns to a Jewish custom of public mourning which signals the gravity of the situation to everyone.

> He tore his clothes, put on sackcloth and ashes, and went out into the midst of the city and wailed loudly and bitterly. And he came as far as the king's gate, for no one was to enter the king's gate clothed in sackcloth.
> Esther 4:1–2

Mordecai eventually sends a message to Esther, begging her to take action, and she replies not as the powerful Queen of Persia but as his vulnerable cousin Hadassah, a marginalized orphan girl who hasn't seen the king in a month. Feeling neglected and rejected, she doubts her own power and fails to recognize the influence she truly holds as queen. She has forgotten who she really is.

Mordecai discerns her self-limiting mindset and knows it's up to him to help his cousin embrace the powerful position she holds in the empire: She *must* let go of her past and stop replaying old tapes. She must recall who she *is* and do what she **can do**. What she **must do**. To address her impostor syndrome, her cousin delivers a prophetic truth:

> For if you keep silent at this time, relief and deliverance will rise for the Jews from another place, but you and your father's family will perish. Who knows? Perhaps you have come to royal dignity for just such a time as this.
> Esther 4:14

Esther understands more than anyone the precarious position she is in: If she appears before the king without being summoned, she **could** be killed; however, if she doesn't see him soon, she 💯 **will** be—along with thousands of others.

It's in this moment we witness Esther's transformation from a girl *taking* orders to a woman *giving* them.

As the **Queen of Persia**, she will use the power she has and bravely step into the role she was created for:

PEOPLE PROTECTOR.

Queen Esther commands her cousin to organize a three-day fast among all the Jews living in Susa, specifying that neither food nor drink be consumed during this period; she and her maids will do the same. This act of solidarity signals her unwavering commitment to **ALL** Jews, not just those from their own tribe of Benjamin.[3]

Once the fast is completed, the queen is prepared mentally and spiritually to approach the king; however, her physical appearance could use some attention. She freshens up, dons her royal robes, and perhaps, dabs on his favorite perfume. 😉

In stark contrast to Vashti who risked her life by refusing to appear before the king when summoned, Esther will risk her life by appearing before the very same man uninvited and unannounced.

When the timing is right, the queen gathers her wits and courageously enters the inner court of the palace, directly across from the king's hall, hoping he will invite her into his presence. Fortunately, she doesn't have to wait long.

> As soon as the king saw Queen Esther standing in the court, she won his favor, and he held out to her the golden scepter that was in his hand. Then Esther approached and touched the top of the scepter.
> Esther 5:2

Now, with the initial tensions eased, the conversation can begin. In a genius move, Queen Esther invites both her husband and Haman to a private banquet—one she's *already* prepared for them.

IS SHE BEING ADVISED?

The intention behind Esther's invitation suggests she might be collaborating with the royal staff. Remember Hegai the Eunuch? They were instrumental in helping Esther adjust to harem life and in securing the king's favor during the competition. Could their bond have extended into her reign as queen?

Although Hegai is not mentioned at this point in the story, Esther's ability to navigate complex Persian palace etiquette and secure the king's favor again—despite breaking the law—hints that she might be receiving advice from someone. My guess is it's from Hegai.

Regardless of whose idea it is to invite the king and Haman to a private banquet, with the food already prepared and ready to eat, it's brilliant. Because. Men. And food. 😂

IF YOU FEED THEM, THEY WILL COME.

It's during this private banquet that Queen Esther reignites her influence with King Ahasuerus, reminding him why he chose to marry her in the first place. Additionally, this intimate setting provides the perfect opportunity for her to invite both men to an encore banquet the next day. I wonder where she slept that night? 😍 😉

It's during their second private banquet, in a courageous act of vulnerability, that Queen Esther reveals her ethnicity: She is, from birth, a Jew.

Haman feels as if a bomb has just dropped in his lap, but the king, oblivious as always, responds lightly, "Hmm, interesting. Now, please pass the hummus."

It's in this moment that Haman realizes the precarious position he is in. His vengeful, empire-wide order to annihilate all the Jews has inadvertently included the king's new wife. Do you think he's starting to sweat yet?

All this, and King Ahasuerus is still **ignorant** to what's going on. He has yet to make the connection between Haman's evil edict and Esther's heritage.

> *You might recall that when Haman originally approached the king with his evil plan, he never actually divulged the identity of the people he wanted to eradicate—he simply described them as people the king should "not tolerate" in his empire. It's mind boggling the king would trust Haman so unquestioningly.*

Recognizing her revelation has not yet landed with the king, Esther "queen-splains" that it is, in fact, *her* people who have been targeted for annihilation by Haman's horrific plan.

Disturbed by this, King Ahasuerus steps out of the room to collect his thoughts; eventually, he puts two and two together. Re-entering the space to rejoin the conversation, he is shocked to see Haman accosting his wife—and that straw breaks this camel's back. The king immediately orders the swift execution of his once-trusted officer, and it happens **FAST**! Boom. Done. 💀

Later, when Esther reveals that her cousin Mordecai is the man who raised her, King Ahasuerus elevates him to Haman's recently vacated position, and just like that, Mordecai takes charge of Haman's estate in Susa.

Seems like a happy ending. All's well that ends well, right? **Not exactly**.

BUT WAIT...THERE'S MORE!

Although Haman is dead, his plan to annihilate the Jews throughout Persia is very much **alive**, thanks to his use of the king's signet ring on the decree. Haman's **pogrom** is still being proclaimed in every province. When Esther realizes the threat against her people remains active, she knows **exactly** what to do.

Side Note: A "pogrom" is a violent riot aimed primarily at the massacre or persecution of an ethnic or religious group, particularly one aimed at Jews.

This time, there are no pep talks. No strategy sessions. No fasts. No private banquets.

Queen Esther finds the king and falls at his feet in tears, pleading with him to rescind Haman's edict and save her people. He extends the golden scepter again; however, that's all he can do. Under Persian law, his hands are tied:

Ancient Egyptian signet ring.

For an edict written in the name of the king and sealed with the king's ring CANNOT be revoked.
Esther 8:8b (emphasis mine)

Aware of the limitations *and* loop holes in Persian law, King Ahasuerus takes initiative for the first time in the entire narrative by offering a workaround: The King authorizes Queen Esther and Mordecai to craft a new decree and seal it with his signet ring.

This means that although Haman's edict could not be rescinded, it *could* effectively be rendered <u>powerless</u>, thanks to the one ring that rules them all.

Finally in a position to make a real difference, Mordecai writes a royal decree that effectively neutralizes Haman's deadly plan. In it, he decrees that all Jews throughout the Persian Empire are allowed to defend themselves on the day Haman had designated for their annihilation, and they are authorized to kill their enemies and seize their possessions.

According to the ninth chapter of *Esther*, the Jews kill thousands, but choose not to take any plunder (*See Side Note*). Immediately following these days of reckoning, they take time to rest and then, later, celebrate their survival and victory. The celebration happens organically and is a natural response to the relief they feel from the threat of annihilation.

Everything in the narrative has been building up to what happens next.

PURIM HOLIDAY

As Queen Esther reflects on the profound significance of recent events so she establishes a new feast to mark the Jews' triumph over Haman's evil plan.

Because. Parties. And Persia.

Starting with Esther's feast, and continuing annually to this day, Jews worldwide have celebrated the **FEAST OF PURIM e**very March for nearly 2,500 years!

Side Note:
Although Esther and Mordecai's new edict effectively prevents a Jewish genocide, it nonetheless results in the deaths of more than 75,000 people who had acted on Haman's original orders or otherwise expressed their hatred for the Jews in Persia. This part of the story is often overlooked; however, it is recorded in *Esther* to show the harsh realities and complexities of ancient political power struggles and the profound impact of divine justice as perceived by the Jewish people. The narrative invites reflection on the difficult choices and moral consequences faced by communities under threat, emphasizing the theme of survival against overwhelming odds and the celebration of unexpected deliverance. It serves as a stark reminder of the costs of conflict and the weight of decisions made in times of crisis.

Annual Purim parties are a lot of fun and include noise makers, costumes, and sweet treats. One special Purim treat is the Hamantaschen cookie (*pictured below).* Did you notice the name *Haman* embedded in the name of the cookie?

Hamantaschen are a traditional Jewish pastry characterized by their distinctive three-cornered shape and a sweet filling of poppy seeds or fruit jams. The triangular shape of the cookie is meant to symbolize the hat worn by Haman, and the cookies serve as a poignant reminder of Haman's defeat and Esther's triumph in saving her people.

Consuming these yummy pastries during Purim both reflects a celebratory act of remembrance and serves to reinforce the themes of survival and victory central to the holiday. See the "Endnotes" (p. 168) for a more detailed look at Purim, supplementary articles, and a recipe for Hamantaschen cookies.[4]

Photo of five Jewish children dressed up and ready to head to the annual Purim carnival in the famous Ultra-Orthodox quarter of Jerusalem.

Can you identify Queen Esther and the King?

Esther's legacy stands as a powerful testament to the strength and resilience one can demonstrate by taking significant actions in the service of others, despite difficult circumstances.

Esther's story challenges us to recognize when we've been placed in a position to make a difference, encourages us to seek confirmation and guidance about our next steps, and spurs us to do what we are being directed to do, all the while trusting God will work the outcome for our good.

You can read about Hadassah's total transformation in the book of **Esther**. ✦

Personal Reflections

What stood out to you?

Did reading this chapter prompt further questions?

Look at the cover photo for this chapter and imagine why it was chosen. What do you notice?

Is there a woman in your life who reminds you of **Esther**? Someone who, against all odds, has stepped into her power to protect and lead those around her? Someone who uses her influence and position for the greater good, fearlessly navigating challenges to make a significant impact? Maybe you've seen someone rise with grace and determination to champion the cause of the vulnerable and voiceless?

Consider sending her a quick text, encouraging message, or longer letter to let her know you're thinking of her today. Acknowledge how her strength and resilience inspire you, or share how her standing up for justice has made a difference in your life and community. And consider sharing how she inspires your walk with God.

If the woman you thought of is you, please send a message to the author at: info@valiantwomenofthebible.com so we can bear witness to your story.

MOVIE REVIEW:
ONE NIGHT WITH THE KING

If you've been moved by Queen Esther's story in this chapter, I recommend rounding out your exploration with the film *One Night with the King*. Released in 2006, this movie offers a captivating portrayal of Hadassah's transformation into Queen Esther intricately intertwined with Haman's sinister plot to destroy the Jews.

The historical narrative is woven into a sweet romance, predictable yet pleasant to watch—similar to a Hallmark movie. ❤️ The film introduces a visually imaginative symbol of Hadassah's Jewish heritage which serves as a powerful motif throughout the narrative, underscoring her deep-rooted identity and commitment to her people.

The film not only romanticizes Esther's story but also poignantly captures her critical dilemma—breaking the law by appearing unsummoned before the king. This act of bravery sets up the climax of the film and offers a compelling visualization of Esther's strategy that not only saves her people but also solidifies her as an influential partner to the king.

With a brief acknowledgment of the days of reckoning and flashes of the first Purim celebration, *One Night with the King* ends the same way it began, honoring the Jewish people for their enduring spirit and resilience in the face of adversity.

One Night with the King is available to watch on many streaming services and free on YouTube®:
https://youtu.be/r4saPofrlbA

Note: This is not a paid advertisement. It's my personal recommendation.

DIGGING DEEPER

Something you may have already noticed is how prevalent the palace parties, private banquets, and feasts are in this narrative. One thing is for certain: The Persians know how to par-tay!

The book of *Esther* is written in a format which proves the inspiration of Scripture extends far beyond the mere words on the page. It includes thoughtful structure, the use of literary devices, thematic elements, symbolism, and nuance. This article will explore how the writer of *Esther* used both words and structure to communicate a clear message.

The book of *Esther* records seven feasts and banquets: Structurally, *Esther* is "book-ended" with two massive celebrations. The first of which is a six-month celebration:

1. The story opens at the end of a spectacular 180-day banquet held for the all the king's nobles and officials, the military leaders of Persia and Media, the princes, and the nobles of 127 provinces throughout the Achaemenid Persian Empire. Why? It was important to the king to show off his vast wealth to the ruling class.

Following the first "book end" celebrations, there are a number of events where people gather to enjoy a meal together:

2. A grand celebration for "all the people in Susa" regardless of rank or ethnicity

3. A separate feast hosted by the queen exclusively for women

4. Esther's coronation feast celebrating her new position as Queen of the Persian Empire

5. The first intimate banquet Queen Esther has prepared for the King and Haman (ready to eat)

6. The second intimate banquet the following day with Queen Esther with the same guests

The second "book end" celebration involves the establishment of Purim.

7. The narrative closes at the start of a new tradition of feasting and celebration called Purim. It was established as an annual feast to remember "*the time when the Jews got relief from their enemies, and as the month when their sorrow was turned into joy and their mourning into a day of celebration*" (Esther 9:22a).

Purim is the seventh and final feast in *Esther*. Since we know that in the Bible, the number seven symbolizes completeness and perfection, then it's easy to see how the establishment of this annual feast is the book's climactic finale.

But there's more to this story than feasting—there's also FASTING.

Esther's call for a three-day fast interrupts the story like the screeching of a needle across a record brings the music to a sudden stop—it grabs our attention.

The fast clearly contrasts with the hustle and bustle of life in Susa, and creates a dramatic pause in the narrative where the gravity of the situation at hand can be contemplated: a pending genocide.

Free from the distractions and interruptions that accompany royal mealtimes, Esther is able to focus. Get clear. Listen for God's voice. And seek wise counsel from trusted confidants.

In the silence and solemnity of her fast, supported by her attendants and in solidarity with the Jews in Susa, Queen Esther finds the clarity and direction she needs to undertake the most significant and risky action of her reign.

This sharp contrast between feasting and fasting illustrates the importance of seeking the Lord's direction before making big decisions. It underscores the value of intentionally slowing down, clearing away the clutter in our minds (and stomachs!), and getting quiet so we can discern God's guidance. When we rush into action without first seeking the Lord, we risk creating unnecessary complications, drama, and chaos.

As you can see, when we take time to dive deeper into Scripture—to look past the words on the page and appreciate the literary structure, symbolism, and context—we are equipped to uncover rich insights and wisdom. This, in turn, shapes how we interpret the passage. God blesses our efforts through the Holy Spirit who opens our eyes to depths and complexities we would otherwise miss.

Literary analysis is just one of the many important aspects of responsible Bible study.

UNNAMED WOMEN

Throughout this book, we've explored the stories of twenty-two remarkable women *called by name* in the Hebrew Bible. However, numerous *unnamed* women also demonstrate profound faith, wisdom, courage, and loyalty during challenging times. This page highlights five such women and offers a glimpse into their significant, albeit often overlooked, contributions to biblical history. I encourage you to dig into their stories using your favorite Bible study resources and the interpretative skills you've honed on this journey.

❖ **JOB'S WIFE (Job 2:9-10 and 40:10-17)**
Job's wife is introduced to us during a moment of extreme despair. In the middle of their suffering, and at the end of her wits, she suggests Job should just, "Curse God and die!" Her story is a poignant reminder of the human struggle with faith and integrity under duress. Despite her brief speaking role in the narrative, she never leaves Job's side. She stays with him through it all, mourning the loss of her children and their livelihood. She and Job eventually rebuild their lives and have many more children together including three *named* daughters who inherit land when Job dies.

❖ **THE DAUGHTERS OF ZELOPHEHAD (Numbers 27:1-11)**
These sisters are bold advocates for a woman's rights, successfully petitioning for changes to inheritance laws in Israel. Their story highlights the importance of women's agency and legal recognition in their community.

❖ **THE WIDOW OF ZAREPHATH (1 Kings 17:8-24)**
This widow exemplifies remarkable faith and hospitality during a severe famine by providing for the prophet Elijah. Her trust in God's provision results in miraculous sustenance and the resurrection of her son, showcasing her profound faith and resilience.

❖ **THE SHUNAMMITE WOMAN (2 Kings 4:8-37)**
Known for her great hospitality and faith, the Shunammite woman's interactions with Elisha lead to the miraculous birth and resurrection of her son. Her story is a testament to the power of faith and God's responsiveness to the faithful.

❖ **THE WISE WOMAN OF ABEL (2 Samuel 20:14-22)**
This wise woman effectively negotiates the safety of all the inhabitants of her city by orchestrating the death of a single rebel leader. Her strategic and brave actions save her city from destruction and highlight the impact of wise leadership.

Slow down, take your time, and really consider each of these women's experiences in their historical and cultural contexts. Explore the relevant Scripture passages more deeply, and apply the analytical and reflective techniques modeled in this book to uncover more about them. Then share what you've learned with a friend.

chapter eighteen

Reclaimed

VALIANT WOMEN

"The Lord is near to all who call on him,
to all who call on him in truth."
Psalm 145:18

Reclaimed

For too long, the lives and contributions of women in the Hebrew Bible have been overshadowed, oversimplified, or overlooked. Through this concentrated exploration, we have brought their stories, in all their nuance and complexity, back out into the light.

 We have honored women's contributions to the biblical narrative and reclaimed their rightful place in our collective memory.

We began our study near the trail head of creation at the moment God created the first humans on the planet, each bearing His image. We saw how He fashioned the second human from the same substance as the first so they could relate to each other and experience life together in a way that no other creatures could.

EVE was curious, brave, and persuasive. In the garden, where she and Adam ate from the tree of knowledge of good and evil, the two were each held accountable for their individual actions. Eve became the world's first wife and mother, and when her children had children of their own, she became the original bubbe, safta, nana, yaya, granny, or mimi. 😉

The narratives of **SARAH**, **HAGAR**, **RACHEL**, and **LEAH** brought us into the heart of the family, where a wife's struggle with infertility was addressed through the ancient custom of forced surrogacy. This human-created solution often resulted in generational trauma. Yet, we also witnessed how God's timing and provision could redeem even the most painful situations. 🙌

We met two Egyptian "rebel" midwives **SHIPHRAH** and **PUAH**, who worked to save the lives of newborn Hebrew boys. They defied the pharaoh's deadly decree, demonstrating the power of moral courage, and God blessed them each with children of their own.

We held our breath when **JOCHEBED** placed her baby in a basket on the Nile, and cheered when her daughter **MIRIAM** reunited them. We witnessed Miriam lead the women in dance after crossing the Red Sea, and learn a tough lesson in the wilderness.

When the Canaanite sex worker, **RAHAB**, prophesied to two Hebrew spies that their invasion of Jericho would succeed and then negotiated for the protection of her family, we sat in awe. Learning she was King David's great-great grandma was icing on the cake!

SHEERAH blew our minds by building three cities in the hill country of Ephraim during the Iron Age, two of which remain. Beth Horon was significant enough to be included in the ancient Egyptian Shishak Inscription.

The intertwined stories of **NAOMI**, **RUTH**, and **ORPAH** reminded us how unpredictable life can be, and reassured us that God is more than able to heal our heartbreaks and provide opportunities for renewal. We also witnessed the value of friendship and the power of a strong sisterhood with the women in Naomi's hometown, as well as her special bond with Ruth.

We were totally impressed with **DEBORAH**, the only female judge named in the Hebrew Bible. Not only was she a prophet and a wife, but her strategic guidance and prophetic leadership also proved pivotal to the Israelites' victory in a battle against the Canaanites.

We were caught a little off-guard when **JAEL** offered shelter to the commander of the Canaanite army, but relieved (and a bit stunned) when she reached for a tent peg and hammer to kill him. Her actions fulfilled a prophecy and helped nail down the Israelites' victory.

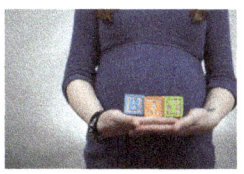

Our hearts broke for **HANNAH**, who, though loved by her husband, was emotionally tormented by his other wife. We prayed with her at the temple in Shiloh and rejoiced when she conceived her first child. We witnessed Hannah keeping her vow to the Lord, moving her son to the temple and creating a new little robe for him each year as a symbol of her love.

We winced as **BATHSHEBA** endured unwanted advances from the king and then carried his baby to full term. We cried with her as she mourned her husband's death, and later grieved the loss of her first child. Eventually, we saw her rise from the ashes of tragedy to become a formidable force in shaping the Davidic Dynasty and securing her son Solomon's ascension to the throne.

Anxiously, we watched as **JEHOSHEBA** quietly made her way through the palace to rescue her baby nephew from her stepmother's murderous rampage, heroically preserving the line of David. Six years later, we celebrated with her at the Temple when the precious little boy she saved was anointed King of Judah.

When King Josiah sent his envoys to seek a prophet of the LORD, and they arrived at **HULDAH**'s house, we couldn't help but smile from ear to ear. 😁 Learning about the important role she played as the first person to officially declare a written text as the Word of God made us sit up a little taller. The fact that God chose a woman for this crucial act cannot be overstated.

We cheered for **VASHTI** when she refused to be paraded as a trophy wife on the final day of her husband's banquet. We admired her strong sense of self-worth and her willingness to risk everything to preserve her dignity. And we understood that,

although she was removed from her royal position, she ultimately achieved what she wanted: not to be paraded as a trophy wife for the king's ego.

Finally, we met **HADASSAH**, also known as Queen **ESTHER**, who succeeded Vashti on the throne. We observed her transformation from a Jewish virgin to a Persian Queen, mastering the complexities of Persian court life while never forgetting where she came from. Her strategic abilities and incredible courage really shone through when she overcame her fears and orchestrated a bold plan to save her people from annihilation. Through her efforts, she not only thwarted a grave injustice but also established the Feast of Purim, a celebration of deliverance that continues to be joyously observed by Jews worldwide today.

Throughout this book, we've been on an emotional roller coaster with high highs and low lows. We've felt the pain of loss and the joy in a miracle. Every woman made a specific and meaningful contribution to the biblical narrative. Each was unique. No one was like the other, and yet, the throughline of courage, grit, and faith was easy to see.

As we reflect on our journey through the oldest books in the Bible, we see a clear pattern with the Lord: He consistently reveals Himself to women from all walks of life and in various circumstances, empowering each one in unique ways not only to fulfill His purposes on earth but also to realize her full potential.

Always has. Still does. Never stopped.

Did you catch that? He always has. He still does. He never stopped. God *still* reveals Himself to women and empowers us to do what He's called us to do. He doesn't always protect us from the challenges that come our way—that's how we grow and develop—but He does see us through them and work everything for our good, because we love Him.

Your dedication to learn about these valiant women—and share what you've learned with others—is helping us reclaim their stories. And this reclamation project extends beyond merely recognizing their names; it's a restoration of dignity and a celebration of their enduring impact on the biblical narrative.

I hope you've found a new source of inspiration and strength, and I hope you reached out to at least one person who has impacted your life—to lift them up and encourage them during these challenging and divisive times.

And I hope you have realized how very much God loves **YOU**, exactly as you are. You have a unique purpose on this planet, and **NOTHING** can stop you from accomplishing it. 🧡

BUT WAIT... *THERE'S MORE!* ✉️

As you know, this is the first volume of a two-volume set. The next volume will delve into the lives of New Testament women, from Elizabeth to Eunice. We'll explore the expanding trajectory of women's roles in daily life, Jesus' ministry, and the early church. Look for *Valiant Women of the Bible, Volume Two: From Elizabeth to Eunice* in early 2025.

Sign-up to be notified when the book is available on the website: <u>valiantwomenofthebible.com</u>.

ACKNOWLEDGMENTS

First and foremost, I want to thank God for inspiring me to write this book and providing the stamina to bring this project to completion. Thank you for gifting me with an extra dose of curiosity, a detail-oriented personality, and a deep love for the Bible and its history.

Next, I offer the most sincere gratitude to my beloved husband, John. You have always encouraged me to be myself, study the Bible, and share what I've learned. You're my biggest fan, and I would never have written this book without your constant support and gifts of "alone time" so I could focus. And thanks for all the date nights at Chile Rojo, because Mexican food is life! 🌮

I'm grateful to our one and only child. ZZ, thanks for all the time you invested listening to various chapters and reading through rough drafts. Your thoughtful questions and candid, constructive feedback has made the book more accessible to everyone. (And thanks for reminding me to breathe!) ❤️

To my mom and dad, thank you for raising me to love the Lord and the Bible, and continuing to pray for me every single day. This book is as much a part of your legacy as it is mine, and I hope it makes you proud (in a humble kind of way). 😉

To my dear sisters, Shannon and Michelle. You have supported me for decades by praying for me, encouraging me, and supporting me during the tough times. Your helpful critiques throughout this process have been super valuable. Thanks for the extra efforts during the home stretch and the last-minute proofreading. Shannon, I'm especially grateful for your candid feedback on the cover.

To my mother-in-law, Ruth Harrington, and my father-in-law of blessed memory, Clint. Your constant encouragement for me to "use your gift of teaching the Bible" means a lot to me.

To my brother-in-Christ in Kenya, Benson Mosor. Thank you for your constant encouragement and prayers over the years. You are special to me, and I'm so glad God brought you into my life.

To my volunteer proofreaders: Monika Traeger (emails), Amy Day (bio), Dr. Jenny Rain (ALL the chapters), and Fatima Sadaf Saied (chapter on Hagar).Thank you for donating your time to offer feedback on the women and research included in this book. Jenny, this book is better because of your questions, insights, and typo-super-sleuthing, AND—your unbridled enthusiasm for this project was oxygen in my lungs on the toughest days!

To my accountability partners, Dr. Paula C. Perez and Judy Mott-Butler, thank you for strongly encouraging me to write this book NOW. I'm so grateful God brought us into each other's lives and how He continues to strengthen our friendship as we build our businesses for His glory. And Paula, my "sister from another mister," thank you for helping me navigate self-publishing. 🙌

To my niece, Savannah. Thank you for allowing me to use a photo of your son when he was three-years old for the chapter on Hannah. He is so smart, funny, and talented. I love my little great nephew!

To my dear friend Jasmin, thank you for allowing me to use a newborn photo of your baby boy for the chapter on Hannah. I'm so glad I got to meet him in person! He's such a cutie pie!

To my long-time friends who have encouraged me to follow God's calling in my life, wherever it leads: Tina Bartlett and Maria Gottschalk. Although we don't see each other as often as we used to, your consistent support over the course of many, many years means the world to me.

To Pete and Diane Smith, thank you for being so supportive of my writing journey, and for being such great neighbors. So glad God brought you into our lives!

I want to give a special thank you to the counselors and coaches who have helped me release the emotional, spiritual, mental, and physical baggage I've carried for far too long. I especially want to thank my health coach, Stephanie Read. I'm so grateful for you! Thanks for helping me reclaim and improve my health one step at a time.

I'd also like to thank the one and only Beth Moore, Founder of Living Proof Ministries, for her pioneering spirit, relentless dedication to the Lord and His Word. Thank you for modeling the life of a valiant woman of God. For being more loyal to Him than any man-made institution. I am so grateful for you.

To Mr. Tye Tribbett: I'm so grateful Amazon Music shuffled you into my playlist last year, as your work has been playing nonstop ever since, providing the soundtrack of my life, especially as "I walk by faith, and not by sight." 🎵

Finally, to the Wambi brothers, Kenneth and Isaac, who run the Rhino Ripple Children's Ministry in Jinja, Uganda. You guys inspire me every day, and I pray that the Lord continues to provide you with **everything** you need to serve all the children in your care. Your need is great, but so is our God! To learn more about the tremendous need at Rhino Ripple Children's Ministry, scan the QR code or visit their website at https://rhinoripple.org. All the funds donated go to provide essentials, clean water, food, shelter, clothing, and education for the children. 🍃

INDEX OF ENDNOTES

INTRODUCTION

1   "Valiant," Merriam-Webster.com Dictionary, Merriam-Webster, **bit.ly/vwb-definition**. Accessed 26 Apr. 2024.

2   Zalman Goldstein and Chaim Fogelman. "Eshet Chayil." *Chabad.org,* **bit.ly/vwb-ec**. Accessed 26 Apr. 2024.

3   Wilda C. Gafney, *Womanist Midrash: A Reintroduction to the Women of the Torah and the Throne* (Westminster John Knox Press, 2017), 3.

CHAPTER 1: EVE

1   Henry Wansbrough, *New Jerusalem Study Bible* (Doubleday, 1985), 19.

2   Patricia Wilson-Kastner, *Faith, Feminism, & the Christ* (Fortress Press, 1983). Out of print.

3   Jo Saxton, "Ezer Kenegdu." *Jo Saxton*, 13 May 2009, www.josaxton.com/notes/2009/05/13/ezer-kenegdu. Archived.

4   Carolyn Custis James, "The Ezer-Kenegdo: Ezer Unleashed," *FaithGateway*, **bit.ly/vwb-custis**. Accessed 28 Feb. 2024.

5   Herbert Edward Ryle, "Genesis," *Cambridge Bible for Schools and Colleges* (Cambridge University Press, 1921), **bit.ly/vwb-gen2**. Accessed 28 Feb. 2024.

6   Elaine H. Pagels. *Adam, Eve, and the Serpent* (Penguin Random House, 1990).

CHAPTER 2: SARAH

1   "Abram Desires an Heir." *Tabletalk Magazine*, 2 Aug. 2006, **bit.ly/vwb-tabletalk** Accessed 14 July 2024.

2   Eliyahu Lizorkin-Eyzenberg and Jim Stowe. "What's the Difference Between Abram/Sarai and Abraham/Sarah?" *Israel Bible Center*, 27 July 2023, **bit.ly/vwb-sarai**.

CHAPTER 3: HAGAR

1   Tikva Frymer-Kensky, updated by Tamar Kamionkowski, "Hagar: Bible," *The Shalvi/Hyman Encyclopedia of Jewish Women*, 23 June 2021, Jewish Women's Archive, **bit.ly/vwb-jwa-hagar**. Accessed 20 Dec. 2023.

2   "Hajj and Hagar," *Women's Islamic Initiative in Spirituality & Equality*, 18 Nov. 2020, **bit.ly/vwb-wise-hagar**.

3   Ibid.

CHAPTER 4: RACHEL & LEAH

1   Edith Deen, *All the Women of the Bible* (Harper & Ross, 1959), 30.

2   Zev Farber. "How Is It Possible that Jacob Mistakes Leah for Rachel?" *TheTorah. Com*, 2017, **bit.ly/vwb-farber**.

3   Susan Niditch. "Genesis." *Women's Bible Commentary, Third Edition: Revised and Updated* (Westminster/John Knox Press, 2012), 39.

SPOTLIGHT: THE WOMB SLAVE

1   Wilda C. Gafney, *Womanist Midrash: A Reintroduction to the Women of the Torah and the Throne* (Westminster John Knox Press, 2017), 76-80.

2   Frymer-Kensky, Tikva. "Patriarchal Family Relationships and Near Eastern Law." *The Biblical Archaeologist*, vol. 44, no. 4, 1981, pp. 209–14. *JSTOR*, **https://doi.org/10.2307/3209666**. Accessed 20 July 2024.

CHAPTER 5: SHIPHRAH & PUAH

1   Flavius Josephus and William Whiston, "The Antiquities of the Jews, 2.201–2.237," *The Genuine Works of Flavius Josephus: The Jewish Historian* (1737), Section 2:206-207, **bit.ly/vwb-josephus-206**.

2   Ana Bonnheim and David Spinrad, "The First Heroes of Exodus (*D'Var Torah* by A.B.; *Daver Acher* by D.S.)," *Reform Judaism*, Jan. 2017, **bit.ly/vwb-midwives**.

CHAPTER 6: JOCHEBED & MIRIAM

1   Carol Meyers, "Jochebed: Bible," *Shalvi/Hyman Encyclopedia of Jewish Women,* 20 Mar. 2009, *Jewish Women's Archive*, **bit.ly/vwb-jwa-jochebed**. Accessed 19 Dec. 2023.

2   Peter Unseth, "Hebrew Kush: Sudan, Ethiopia, or Where?" *Africa Journal of Evangelical Theology* 18, no. 2 (1999): 143-159.

3   "Luxor: Merneptah Stele - overview," The Land of Israel / Palestine: Image Database, University of Michigan, **bit.ly/vwb-stele**. Accessed June 1, 2024.

CHAPTER 7: RAHAB

1   Edith Deen, *All the Women of the Bible* (Harper & Ross, 1959).

CHAPTER 8: SHEERAH

1   David Frankel, "The Book of Chronicles and the Ephraimites that Never Went to Egypt," *TheTorah.com*, 2015, **bit.ly/vwb-sheerah1**.

2   Wilda C. Gafney, *Womanist Midrash: A Reintroduction to the Women of the Torah and the Throne* (Westminster John Knox Press, 2017).

3   Ernest Alfred Wallis Budge, "Bat Huarn," *An Egyptian Hieroglyphic Dictionary* (John Murray, 1920), Uploaded 1 Jan. 1970, **bit.ly/vwb-budge**.

CHAPTER 9: NAOMI, RUTH, & ORPAH

1   Oprah Winfrey, "Interview with the Academy of Achievement," **bit.ly/vwb-oprah**.

2   In various Bible passages, 'feet' is used as a euphemism (see Exodus 4:25; Deuteronomy 27:20; 1 Samuel 24:3; 2 Samuel 11:8; Isaiah 7:20; Ezekiel 16:25). This suggests that Ruth's proposal to Boaz also included a direct romantic or sexual overture. His invitation for her to stay afterward indicates his interest. Scholars are divided on the exact interpretation of this scene, often due to differing views on the nuances of ancient Hebrew language as well as religious and cultural contexts. Regardless of these debates, it is clear that Ruth and Boaz were united in marriage shortly after this encounter. Read Israel Drazin's article, "What Did Ruth and Boaz Do on the Threshing Floor?", *Times of Israel*, 17 July 2017. **bit.ly/vwb-drazin**.

3   Ilona Rashkow, "Ruth: The Discourse of Power and the Power of Discourse," *Feminist Companion to Ruth,* edited by Athalya Brenner (Sheffield Academic Press, 1993), 39.

4   Adrien J. Bledstein, "Female Companionships: If the Book of Ruth Were Written

by a Woman..." *Feminist Companion to Ruth,* edited by Athalya Brenner (Sheffield Academic Press, 1993), 123-127.

5   Phyllis Trible, "Ruth: Bible," *Shalvi/Hyman Encyclopedia of Jewish Women*, 31 Dec. 1999, Jewish Women's Archive, **bit.ly/vwb-jwa-ruth**. Accessed 23 Jan. 2024.

6   Robert L. Hubbard, Jr., *New International Commentary on the New Testament: The Book of Ruth* (Wm. B. Eerdmans Publishing Company, 1988), 271.

7   Rachel Adelman, "Seduction and Recognition in the Story of Judah and Tamar and the Book of Ruth," *Nashim: A Journal of Jewish Women's Studies & Gender Issues*, no. 23, edited by Rachel S. Harris (Spring–Fall 2012), 98.

8   Ibid., 99.

9   Joseph Lukowski, "There is a son born to Naomi, but it's a grandson. What's up with that?" *Hermeneutics Stack Exchange,* 2013, **bit.ly/vwb-lukowsk**i.

10   Eunny Lee, "Ruth," *Women's Bible Commentary*, edited by Carol A. Newsom, Sharon H. Ringe, and Jacqueline E. Lapsley, 3rd ed. (Westminster John Knox Press, 2012), 148-149.

CHAPTER 10: DEBORAH

1   Edith Deen, *All the Women of the Bible* (Harper & Ross, 1959), 69.

CHAPTER 11: JAEL

1   Tikva Frymer-Kensky and Caryn Tamber-Rosenau, "Yael: Bible," *Shalvi/Hyman Encyclopedia of Jewish Women,* 23 June 2021, Jewish Women's Archive, **bit.ly/vwb-jwa-jael**. 15 Jan. 2024.

2   Credit to Jools Lebron who coined the phrase "very mindful, very demure." I had already used the word "demure" here before their TikTok video went viral. And since I'm a pop culture geek, it just made sense to include the full phrase here.

3   Tamar Kadari, "Yael Wife of Heber The Kenite: Midrash and Aggadah," *Shalvi/Hyman Encyclopedia of Jewish Women,* 31 Dec. 1999, *Jewish Women's Archive*, **bit.ly/vwb-jwa-jael2**. Accessed 26 Jan. 2024.

CHAPTER 12: HANNAH

1   "1 Samuel 1," *Pulpit Commentary*, *BibleHub.com*, **bit.ly/vwb-pulpit-1sam1**. Accessed 26 July 2024.]

CHAPTER 13: BATHSHEBA

1   J. Kenneth Kuntz, "Bathsheba," *Dictionary of Bible and Religion*, edited by William H. Gentz (Abingdon Press, 1986), 110-111.

2   Jo Ann Hackett, "1 and 2 Samuel," *Women's Bible Commentary*, edited by Carol A. Newsom, Sharon H. Ringe, and Jacqueline E. Lapsley, 3rd ed. (Westminster John Knox Press, 2012), 159.

3   Tikva Frymer-Kensky, *Reading the Women of the Bible: A New Interpretation of Their Stories* (New York: Knopf Doubleday Publishing Group, Kindle Edition), 147. "When Bathsheba purifies herself, she is washing off the impurity that comes with all sexual relations, even licit ones. In our verse, the phrase does not refer back to the bath that she was taking when she was first introduced, but to postcoital [after sex] purification. The verbal form (present participle) also implies the sequential arrangement: having purified herself, she returned home."

4   Claude Mariottini. "Bathsheba and Her Menstrual Period." *ClaudeMariottini.com*, 23 July 2019. **bit.ly/vwb-bathsheba**. Accessed 27 July 2024.

5   Frymer-Kensky, *Reading the Women of the Bible*, 153: "David has been in the habit of 'gathering' or 'harvesting' the wives of other men. First Ahinoam, who otherwise appears as Saul's wife (1 Sam. 14:50); then Michal, Saul's daughter whom David first married, then left, then took from the weeping Paltiel (2 Sam. 3:14–16); then the newly widowed Abigail, after her husband, Nabal, died of apoplexy (1 Sam. 24:42), and now the newly widowed Bathsheba."

6   Frymer-Kensky, *Reading the Women of the Bible*, 396. Regina Schwartz, as discussed by Tikva Frymer-Kensky, points out that King David's methods of taking wives grew increasingly bold over time. Initially, David married women like Ahinoam and Abigail, who were already widowed, without causing harm to anyone. But as time went on, his actions became more forceful. He took Michal back from her husband, who was left crying, and ultimately, he arranged for Bathsheba's husband to be killed so he could marry her. This shift from taking advantage of opportunities to committing outright violence shows a deepening moral decline in David's character.

7   Hackett, p. 159.

8   For interesting insights about the emotional and spiritual significance of David's actions during the seven days he spent praying and fasting, I highly recommend reading "The Death of David's Son by Bathsheba (II Sam 12:13-25): A Narrative in Context" by Jonathan Jacobs. Vetus Testamentum, vol. 63, no. 4, 2013, pp. 566–76. JSTOR, **http://www.jstor.org/stable/43894068**. Accessed 26 June 2024. Additionally, if you've suffered the death of a child, allow me to recommend a much longer article by preacher/teacher/elder Bob Deffinbaugh who shares your experience. His reflections are both vulnerable, encouraging, and theologically sound: "13. The Death of David's Son (2 Samuel 12:14-31)." Bible.org, 1 June 2004, **https://bit.ly/vwb-deffinbaugh.** Accessed 25 Jun. 2024.

9   Lawrence J. Mykytiuk, Identifying Biblical Persons in Northwest Semitic Inscriptions of 1200-539 B.C.E. (Society of Biblical Literature, 2004), 132.

10 Ibid. Mykytiuk explains, "'The house of David' in this inscription and in the Bible was a dynastic and geopolitical entity referred to as such by the Aramaeans in the characteristic terminology they used for naming such entities of that era. The inscriptional suggestion that David's dynasty ruled Judah meets with biblical affirmation...The house of David was important enough to be recognized internationally and was considered significant enough to be mentioned in a public monument, likely as an enemy whose military power was recognized, so that any leader who could defeat it could justly boast.

CHAPTER 14: JEHOSHEBA

1   Flavius Josephus, "Antiquities of the Jews," *The Works of Flavius Josephus*, Translated by William Whiston, A.M. (John E. Beardsley, 1895), Book 8 Section 398.

2   As recorded in 2 Kings 8:26, Ahaziah was 22 years old at the start of his reign, which aligns with the generational timeline of his family. However, a passage in 2 Chronicles 22:2 presents a conflicting detail, stating that he was 42 years old when he became king. This latter age presents a chronological puzzle, as it would not only make Ahaziah older than his father at the time of the latter's death but also disrupts the logical sequence of the royal lineage. The consensus among scholars is that the age of 42 mentioned in 2 Chronicles is a transcription error made in the process of copying the text over centuries. Thus, the age of 22, as recorded in 2 Kings, is considered the accurate record of Ahaziah's age at his ascension to the throne, fitting neatly into the established historical and familial context.

3   Flavius Josephus. "Antiquities of the Jews" *The Works of Flavius Josephus*. Translated by. William Whiston, A.M. (John E. Beardsley, 1895), Book 9 Section 140b.

4   Most scholars conclude Jehosheba is King Jehoram's daughter by another wife—not Athaliah—since she is identified as the sister of Athaliah's son, not the queen's daughter. Ahaziah was Jehosheba's "brother from another mother." Literally.

CHAPTER 15: HULDAH

1   Nissan Mindel. "Who Was Huldah the Prophetess?" *Chabad.org*, Kehot Publication Society, 2008, **bit.ly/vwb-chabad-huldah**. Accessed 03 Feb. 2023.

2   Edith Deen, *All the Women of the Bible*, (Harper & Ross, 1959), 143.

3   Pulling verses out of their biblical, historical, and cultural contexts to "prove" one's position that God would never call a woman to lead is both irresponsible and oppressive. One of the most basic principles of responsible Bible interpretation, championed by the Reformers, is this: **Scripture interprets Scripture**. This means the whole of Scripture should be used to interpret any part of it, and vice versa. This principle helps prevent "cherry pickers" from selecting only certain verses to make the Bible say something it didn't actually mean. We must interpret Scripture responsibly—within its appropriate historical, cultural, and biblical contexts. To do otherwise isn't just irresponsible, it's damaging and hurtful and could seriously undermine the witness and impact of the church.

CHAPTER 16: VASHTI

1   Alinda Damsma, "The Targums to Esther," *European Judaism: A Journal for the New Europe*, vol. 47, no. 1, 2014, pp. 127–36. *JSTOR*, **bit.ly/vwb-jstor-targums**. Accessed 14 Feb. 2024.

2   "Vashti's Banquet: A New Women's Celebration," *Women's League for Conservative Judaism*, 23 Apr. 2018, **bit.ly/vwb-vashti-banquet**. Accessed 20 Oct. 2023.

3   Sidnie White Crawford, "Esther," *Women's Bible Commentary*, edited by Carol A. Newsom, Sharon H. Ringe, and Jacqueline E. Lapsley, 3rd ed. (Westminster John Knox Press, 2012), 204.

CHAPTER 17: ESTHER

1   History.com Editors, "Persian Empire," HISTORY, A&E Television Networks, 30 May 2023, **bit.ly/vwb-persianempire**. Accessed 20 Mar. 2024.

2   110Jean-Louis Huot, "Xerxes I," Encyclopedia Britannica, 20 Mar. 2024, **bit.ly/vwb-xerxes**. Accessed 30 July 2024.

3   A special thank you to Rabbi Frederick 'Fred' Klein for the insight about Esther's efforts at uniting all the Jews, regardless of their tribe of origin.

4   The name "Purim" comes from the word *pur*, which means "lot" in ancient Persian. The holiday is named after the lots (*purim*, plural of *pur*) that Haman, the villain in the book of *Esther*, cast to determine the day he would carry out his plan to annihilate the Jews of the Persian Empire. As the story goes, Haman decided to destroy the Jews and cast lots to choose the date for this genocide. The holiday itself, however, celebrates the reversal of Haman's evil decree, and marks the Jews' deliverance from their enemies through the interventions of Queen Esther and her cousin Mordecai. Purim is a celebration of survival and victory against all odds, the name serving as a reminder of the ironic twist of fate that led to Haman's downfall instead of the Jewish people's destruction.

> (a) How the "Feast of Purim" got it's name: **bit.ly/vwb-purim101**
> (b) How Purim is currently celebrated: **bit.ly/vwb-gh-purim**
> (c) How to Make Buttery "Hamantaschen Cookies" Recipe: **bit.ly/vwb-cookies**

QUOTED BIBLE VERSES

LIST OF SIDE NOTE TOPICS

SOAPBOX MOMENTS

TIMELINES & FAMILY TREES

HISTORICAL MAPS

BIBLIOGRAPHY

"559. amar." *Bible Hub*, 22 Jan. 2024, **biblehub.com/hebrew/559.htm**.

"802. ishshah." *Bible Hub*, 22 Jan. 2024, **biblehub.com/hebrew/802.htm**.

"2339 chut." *Bible Hub*, 22 Jan. 2024, **biblehub.com/hebrew/2339.htm**.

"5291. naarah." *Bible Hub*, 22 Jan. 2024, **biblehub.com/hebrew/5291.htm**.

"7934. shake." *Bible Hub*, 22 Jan. 2024, **biblehub.com/hebrew/7934.htm**.

"8615 tiqvah." *Bible Hub*, 22 Jan. 2024, **biblehub.com/hebrew/8615.htm**.

"Abarim Publications' Theological Dictionary: Rahab." Abarim Publications, 31 May 2011, last updated 27 June 2024, **bit.ly/vwb-rachab**. Accessed 23 July 2024.

"Abram Desires an Heir." *Tabletalk Magazine*. 2 Aug. 2006. **bit.ly/vwb-tabletalk**. Accessed 14 July 2024.

Adelman, Rachel. "Bathsheba: Bible." *Shalvi/Hyman Encyclopedia of Jewish Women*. 23 June 2021. *Jewish Women's Archive*, **bit.ly/vwb-jwa-bathsheba**, Accessed 20 Mar. 2024.

---. "Seduction and Recognition in the Story of Judah and Tamar and the Book of Ruth," *Nashim: A Journal of Jewish Women's Studies & Gender Issues*, no. 23, Consulting Editor: Rachel S. Harris, (Spring–Fall 2012), pp. 87-109.

"The Annunciation of the Births of John the Baptist and Jesus (Luke 1:5-56)." *Asbury Bible Commentary - Bible Gateway*, The Zondervan Corporation, 1992, **bit.ly/vwb-asbury-ann**.

"Archeologists Dig up King David's Palace." *The Jerusalem Post - JPost.Com*, 18 July 2013, **bit.ly/vwb-jpost-palace**. Accessed 24 May 2024.

"Benson Commentary on the Old and New Testaments." *Benson Commentary on the Old and New Testaments: 1 Samuel*, **bit.ly/vwb-benson-1sam**. Accessed 12 Aug. 2023.

Bledstein, Adrien J. "Female Companionships: If the Book of Ruth Were Written by a Woman..." *Feminist Companion to Ruth*, edited by Athalya Brenner. Sheffield Academic Press, 1993.

Bonnheim, Ana, and David Spinrad. "The First Heroes of Exodus (*D'Var Torah* by A.B.; Daver Acher by D.S.)." *Reform Judaism*, Jan. 2017, **bit.ly/vwb-rj-midwives**.

Brenner, Athalya. "Athaliah: Bible." *Shalvi/Hyman Encyclopedia of Jewish Women*. 31 Dec. 1999. *Jewish Women's Archive*, **bit.ly/vwb-jwa-athaliah**. Accessed 20 Mar. 2024.

Britannica, The Editors of Encyclopedia. "Moabite". *Encyclopedia Britannica*, 19 Jan. 2024, **britannica.com/topic/Moabite**. Accessed 22 March 2024.

---. "Samaritan". *Encyclopedia Britannica*, 7 Feb. 2024, **www.britannica.com/topic/Samaritan**. Accessed 13 March 2024.

---. "Susa". *Encyclopedia Britannica*, 19 Mar. 2024, www.britannica.com/place/Susa. Accessed 21 March 2024.

Budge, Ernest Alfred Wallis. "Bat Huarn." *An Egyptian Hieroglyphic Dictionary*. John Murray, 1920. Uploaded 1 Jan. 1970, bit.ly/vwb-budge. Accessed 20 Mar. 2024.

Camp, Claudia V.. "Huldah: Bible." *Shalvi/Hyman Encyclopedia of Jewish Women*. 31 Dec. 1999. *Jewish Women's Archive*, bit.ly/vwb-jwa-huldah. Accessed 20 Mar. 2024.

Cook, Glenn. "Xerxes I." *Cook Ancestry*, bit.ly/vwb-cook-xerxes. Accessed 22 Mar. 2024.

Cooper, John Charles. "Joash." *The Dictionary of Bible and Religion,* edited by William H. Gentz. Abingdon, 1986, p. 539.

Crawford, Sidnie White. "Esther." *Women's Bible Commentary*, edited by Carol A. Newsom, Sharon H. Ringe, and Jacqueline E. Lapsley, 3rd ed. Westminster John Knox Press, 2012.

Crawford, Sidnie White, and Joshua Aaron Alfaro. "Vashti: Bible." *Shalvi/Hyman Encyclopedia of Jewish Women*, 23 June 2021. *Jewish Women's Archive*, bit.ly/vwb-jwa-vashti. Accessed 20 Mar. 2024.

Curwin, David. "Ish and Isha." *Balashon*, 1 Oct. 2008, bit.ly/vwb-isha.

Damsma, Alinda. "The Targums to Esther." *European Judaism: A Journal for the New Europe*, Vol. 47, No. 1, 2014, pp. 127–36. *JSTOR*, bit.ly/vwb-jstor-targums. Accessed 14 Feb. 2024.

Deen, Edith. *All of the Women of the Bible*. New York, Harper & Ross, 1959.

Deffinbaugh, Bob. "13. The Death of David's Son (2 Samuel 12:14-31)." Bible.org, 1 June 2004, https://bit.ly/vwb-deffinbaugh. Accessed 25 Jun. 2024.

Ditmore, Tammy (2008) "The Pains of Natural Childbirth: Eve's Legacy to Her Daughters," *Leaven*: Vol. 16: Iss. 2, Article 5.

Drazin, Israel. "What Did Ruth and Boaz Do on the Threshing Floor?" *Times of Israel*, 17 July 2017. bit.ly/vwb-drazin. Accessed 20 Mar. 2024.

Eames, Christopher. "Before Boaz and Ruth-Salmon and Rahab?" *Armstrong Institute*, 29 July 2021. bit.ly/vwb-eames. Accessed 20 Mar. 2024.

Farber, Rabbi Dr. Zev. "How Is It Possible That Jacob Mistakes Leah for Rachel?" *TheTorah.Com*, 2017, bit.ly/vwb-farber. Accessed 20 Mar. 2024.

fasi6083. "Safaa and Marwa Mountains in Makkah." *Local Guides Connect*, 31 Jan. 2023, bit.ly/vwb-makkah. Accessed 20 Mar. 2024.

Fink, Todd. "Shiloh: Tabernacle Location, Joshua, Hannah's Prayer, Samuel." *Holy Land Site Ministries*, bit.ly/vwb-hs-shiloh. Accessed 12 Aug. 2023.

Frankel, David. "The Book of Chronicles and the Ephraimites that Never Went to Egypt." *TheTorah.com*, 8 April 2015, rev. 5 March 2024. bit.ly/vwb-sheerah1. Accessed 3 Oct. 2023.

Frymer-Kensky, Tikva, and Caryn Tamber-Rosenau. "Deborah: Bible." *Shalvi/Hyman Encyclopedia of Jewish Women*, 23 June 2021. *Jewish Women's Archive*, bit.ly/vwb-jwa-deborah. Accessed 20 Mar. 2024.

Frymer-Kensky, Tikva. "Hagar: Bible." *Shalvi/Hyman Encyclopedia of Jewish Women*, 23 Jun. 2021 *Jewish Women's Archive*, **bit.ly/vwb-jwa-hagar**. Accessed 20 Mar. 2024.

---. "Rahab: Bible." *Shalvi/Hyman Encyclopedia of Jewish Women*, 23 June 2021. *Jewish Women's Archive*, **bit.ly/vwb-jwa-rahab**. Accessed 20 Mar. 2024.

Frymer-Kensky, Tikva, and Caryn Tamber-Rosenau. "Yael: Bible." *Shalvi/Hyman Encyclopedia of Jewish Women*, 23 June 2021. *Jewish Women's Archive*, **bit.ly/vwb-jwa-jael**. Accessed 20 Mar. 2024.

Gadeloff, David. "How Long Was the Sojourn in Egypt: 210 or 430 Years?" *Jewish Bible Quarterly*, Vol. 44, Issue No. 3, July – September 2016.

Gafney, Wil. "She Built a City: Sheerah the Biblical City-Builder." *The Rev. Wil Gafney, Ph.D. | Womanists Wading in the Word™*. 29 Dec. 2012, **bit.ly/vwb-gafney**. Accessed 20 Mar. 2024.

Gafney, Wilda C. *Womanist Midrash: A Reintroduction to the Women of the Torah and the Throne*. Westminster John Knox Press, 2017.

"Genesis 16:13." *Sefaria*, 2020, **bit.ly/vwb-sefaria-g1613**. Accessed 20 Mar. 2024.

Hackett, Jo Ann. "1 and 2 Samuel." *Women's Bible Commentary*, edited by Carol A. Newsom, Sharon H. Ringe, and Jacqueline E. Lapsley, 3rd ed., Westminster John Knox Press, 2012.

Hamilton, Victor P. *New International Commentary on the Old Testament Series: The Book of Genesis*. William B Eerdmans Publishing Co., n.d.

History.com Editors. "Persian Empire." *HISTORY, A&E Television Networks*. 30 May 2023. **bit.ly/vwb-persianempire**. Accessed 20 Mar. 2024.

Holmes, Mark H. "Xerxes I, The Great King of Persia," 12 Sept. 2012, **bit.ly/vwb-wb-xerxes**. Accessed 20 Mar. 2024.

Holy Land Site, "Shiloh: Tabernacle Location, Joshua, Hannah's Prayer, Samuel," Holy Land Site, **holylandsites.com/shiloh**. Accessed 20 Mar. 2024.

Howard, Cameron B.R. "1 and 2 Kings." *Women's Bible Commentary*, edited by Carol A. Newsom, Sharon H. Ringe, and Jacqueline E. Lapsley, 3rd ed., Westminster John Knox Press, 2012.

Hubbard, Jr. Robert L. *New International Commentary on the New Testament: The Book of Ruth*. William B Eerdmans Publishing Co, 1988.

Huot, Jean-Louis. "Xerxes I." *Encyclopedia Britannica*. 20 Mar. 2024. **bit.ly/vwb-xerxes**. Accessed 30 July 2024.

Jacobs, Jonathan. "The Death of David's Son by Bathsheba (II Sam 12:13-25): A Narrative in Context." *Vetus Testamentum*, vol. 63, no. 4, 2013, pp. 566–76. *JSTOR*, **http://www.jstor.org/stable/43894068**. Accessed 26 June 2024.

James, Carolyn Custis. "Half the Church." Faith Gateway, **bit.ly/vwb-custis**. Accessed 20 Mar. 2024.

Josephus, Flavius, and William Whiston. "The Antiquities of the Jews, 2.201–2.237." *The Genuine Works of Flavius Josephus, the Jewish Historian,*1737, Section 2:206-207, **bit.ly/vwb-josephus-206**. Accessed 20 Mar. 2024.

Jpost.com Staff, "Archeologists Dig Up King David's Palace." *Jerusalem Post*, 18 July 2013, **bit.ly/vwb-jpost-palace**. Accessed 20 Mar. 2024.

Kadari, Tamar. "Yael Wife of Heber The Kenite: Midrash and Aggadah." *Shalvi/Hyman Encyclopedia of Jewish Women*. 31 December 1999. *Jewish Women's Archive*. **bit.ly/vwb-jwa-jael2**. Accessed 26 Jan. 24.

Keil, Carl Fredrich, and Franz Delitzsh. "Biblical Commentary on the Old Testament: Esther." *Internet Sacred Text Archive*, **bit.ly/vwb-kd-esther**. Accessed 29 Oct. 2023.

"Kishon." *Encyclopaedia Judaica*. Encyclopedia.com. **bit.ly/vwb-enc-kishon**. Accessed 18 Mar. 2024.

Klein (Abensohn), Lillian. "Hannah: Bible." *Shalvi/Hyman Encyclopedia of Jewish Women*. 31 Dec. 1999. *Jewish Women's Archive*, **bit.ly/vwb-jwa-hannah**. Accessed 20 Mar. 2024.

Kleinhans, T. J. "Jehoida." *The Dictionary of Bible and Religion,* edited by William H. Gentz. Abingdon Press, 1986, p. 521-522.

Knoppers, Gary. "Excursus: The Genealogies." *The Anchor Bible*, 1st ed., Vol. 12. Doubleday and Company, Inc., 2003.

Labahn, Antje, and Ehud Ben Zvi. "Observations on Women in the Genealogies of 1 Chronicles 1–9." *Biblica*, Vol. 84, 2003, pp. 457-478, **bit.ly/vwb-biblica-v84**. Accessed 25 Jan. 24.

Laffey, Alice L. *An Introduction to the Old Testament: A Feminist Perspective*. Fortress Press, 1988.

Lavee, Moshe, and Shana Strauch-Schick. "The "Egyptian" Midwives." *TheTorah.com*, **www.thetorah.com/article/the-egyptian-midwives**. Accessed 20 Mar. 2024.

Levavi Feinstein , Eve. "Menstruation in the Bible." *Shalvi/Hyman Encyclopedia of Jewish Women*. 23 June 2021. *Jewish Women's Archive*, **bit.ly/vwb-jwa-period**. Accessed on 21 Feb. 24.

Lizorkin-Eyzenberg, Dr. Eliyahu, and Rev. Jim Stowe. "What's the Difference Between Abram/Sarai and Abraham/Sarah?" *Israel Bible Center*. 27 July 2023, **bit.ly/vwb-sarai**. Accessed 20 Mar. 2024.

Lukowski, Joseph. (2013). "There is a son born to Naomi, but it's a grandson. What's up with that?" [Online forum post]. *Hermeneutics Stack Exchange*. **bit.ly/vwb-lukowski**. Accessed 14 Apr. 2024.

"Luxor: Merneptah Stele - overview." *The Land of Israel / Palestine: Image Database*, University of Michigan. Accessed 1 June 2024. **bit.ly/vwb-stele**

Mariottini, Claude. "Bathsheba and Her Menstrual Period." *ClaudeMariottini.com*. 23 July 2019. **bit.ly/vwb-bathsheba**. Accessed 27 July 2024.

---. "Sheerah: A Woman of Distinction." *ClaudeMariottini.com*, **bit.ly/vwb-sheerah2**. Accessed 20 Mar. 2023.

Mark, Joshua J. "The Legend of Sargon of Akkad." *World History Encyclopedia*. 17 Feb. 2023, **bit.ly/vwb-sargon**. Accessed 20 Mar. 2024.

Martin, Ralph P. "Beth-Horon." *The Dictionary of Bible and Religion,* edited by William H. Gentz. Abingdon, 1986, p. 123.

Meyers, Carol. "Jochebed: Bible." *Shalvi/Hyman Encyclopedia of Jewish Women*. 31 December 1999. *Jewish Women's Archive*. **bit.ly/vwb-jwa-jochebed**.

Mindel, Nissan. "Who Was Huldah the Prophetess?" *Chabad.Org*, Kehot Publication Society. **bit.ly/vwb-chabad-huldah**. Accessed 15 Oct. 2023.

Montet, Edouard. "The Discovery of the Deuteronomic Law." *The Biblical World*, Nov. 1910, Volume 36, Number 5. University of Chicago Press, 1910, pp. 316 – 322.

Netchev, Simeon. "The Achaemenid Persian Empire c. 500 BCE." *World History Encyclopedia*. 05 Jul 2022. **bit.ly/vwb-map-persia**. Accessed 28 Oct 2023.

Newsom, Carol A., Sharon H. Ringe, and Jacqueline E. Lapsley. *Women's Bible Commentary*, edited by, 3rd ed. Westminster John Knox Press, 2012.

Niditch, Susan. "Genesis." *Women's Bible Commentary*, edited by Carol A. Newsom, Sharon H. Ringe, and Jacqueline E. Lapsley, 3rd ed., Westminster John Knox Press, 2012.

Orr, James, editor. "Beth-Horon." *International Standard Bible Encyclopedia Online*, Wm. B. Eerdmans Publishing Co., 1939, **bit.ly/vwb-isbe-bethhoron**. Accessed 20 Mar. 2024.

Pagels, Elaine H. *Adam, Eve, and the Serpent*. Penguin Books, 1990.

Rad, Gerhard Von, and Marks John H P. *Genesis. A Commentary*. (Translation by John H. Marks.) Revised Edition. SCM Press, 1972.

Rashkow, Ilona. "Ruth: The Discourse of Power and the Power of Discourse." *Feminist Companion to Ruth,* edited by Athalya Brenner. Sheffield Academic Press, 1993.

Roat, Alyssa. "The Samaritans: Hope from the History of a Hated People." *Bible Study Tools*, Salem Web Network. **bit.ly/vwb-bst-samaritans**.

Ryle, Herbert Edward. "Genesis." *Cambridge Bible for Schools and Colleges*. Cambridge University Press, 1921, **bit.ly/vwb-gen2**. Accessed 28 Feb. 2024.

Saxton, Jo. "Ezer Kenegdu." Jo Saxton, 13 May 2009, www.josaxton.com/notes/2009/05/13/ezer-kenegdu. Page no longer available. Accessed 20 Feb. 2018.

Scholz, Susanne. "Judges." *Women's Bible Commentary, Third Edition: Revised and Updated*. Westminster/John Knox Press, 2012.

Simons, Keith. "The David-Bathsheba Story." *The Useful Bible*. **bit.ly/vwb-useful-bath**, n.d. Accessed 22 Mar. 2024.

Sonessa, Wondimu Legesse. "*Imago Dei* and the Tensions of Ethnic Identity." *Journal of Ecumenical Studies*, Vol. 56, Number 1, Winter 2021, pp. 116-147. JHU Muse, **bit.ly/vwb-sonessa**. Accessed 4 Mar. 2024.

Stewart, Anne W. "Deborah, Jael, and Their Interpreters." *Women's Bible Commentary, Third Edition: Revised and Updated*. Westminster/John Knox Press, 2012.

Strauch-Schick, Shana, and Moshe Lavee. "The 'Egyptian' Midwives." *TheTorah.Com*, 2015, **bit.ly/vwb-tc-midwives**. Accessed 3 Feb. 2024.

Strong's Exhaustive Concordance of the Bible: "2339 chut." *BibleHub.com*. **biblehub.com/hebrew/2339.htm**. Retrieved 22 Jan. 2024.

---. "8615 tiqvah: cord." *BibleHub.com*. **biblehub.com/hebrew/8615.htm**. Retrieved 22 Jan. 2024.

"Susa." UNESCO World Heritage Centre. **bit.ly/vwb-unesco-susa**. Accessed 23 Oct. 2023.

Trible, Phyllis. "Ruth: Bible." *Shalvi/Hyman Encyclopedia of Jewish Women*. 31 December 1999. *Jewish Women's Archive*. **bit.ly/vwb-jwa-ruth**. Accessed 20 Mar. 2024.

Unseth, Peter. "Hebrew Kush: Sudan, Ethiopia, or Where?" A*frica Journal of Evangelical Theology*, vol. 18, no. 2, 1999, pp. 143-159.

"Valiant." Merriam-Webster.com Dictionary, Merriam-Webster, **bit.ly/vwb-definition**. Accessed 26 Apr. 2024.

"Vashti's Banquet: A New Women's Celebration." *Women's League for Conservative Judaism*. 23 Apr. 2018, **bit.ly/vwb-vashti-banquet**. Accessed 5 Feb. 2023.

Walton, John H., and Craig S. Keener. *NRSV Cultural Backgrounds Study Bible: Bringing to Life the Ancient World of Scripture*, Zondervan, 2019.

Wansbrough, Henry. *New Jerusalem Study Bible*. Doubleday, 1985.

Wegner, Josef. "The Magical Birth Brick." *Expedition Magazine,* vol. 48, no. 2 (July, 2006). **bit.ly/vwb-birthbrick**. Accessed 18 Jan. 24.

"What Were the Various Sacrifices in the Old Testament?" *GotQuestions.org*. **bit.ly/vwb-gq-sacrifices**. Accessed 20 Mar. 2024.

Winfrey, Oprah. "Oprah Winfrey Interview." *Academy of Achievement*, Jan. 21, 1991. Archived from the original on 19 Jan. 2016. Retrieved 25 Aug. 2008. **bit.ly/vwb-oprah**. Accessed 20 Mar. 2024.

"Who Was King Ahaziah in the Bible?" *GotQuestions.org*. **bit.ly/vwb-gq-ahaziah**. Accessed 20 Mar. 2024.

Wikipedia Contributors. "Bethoron." *Wikipedia, The Free Encyclopedia*, 19 Feb. 2024, **bit.ly/vwb-wiki-bethoron**. Accessed 20 Feb. 2024.

---. "Jehoram of Judah." *Wikipedia, The Free Encyclopedia*, **bit.ly/vwb-wiki-jehoram**.

---. "Jehosheba." *Wikipedia, The Free Encyclopedia*, **bit.ly/vwb-wiki-jehosheba**.

---. "Nazirite." *Wikipedia, The Free Encyclopedia*, **bit.ly/vwb-wiki-nazirite**.

---. "Sargon of Akkad." *Wikipedia, The Free Encyclopedia*, **bit.ly/vwb-wiki-sargon**.

---. "Susa." *Wikipedia, The Free Encyclopedia*, **bit.ly/vwb-wiki-susa**.

Wilson-Kastner, Patricia. *Faith, Feminism, & the Christ*. Fortress Press, 1983. Out of print.

WISE Muslim Women. "Hajj and Hagar." *WISE Muslim Women*. **bit.ly/vwb-wise-hajj**. Accessed 21 Mar. 2024.

Wong, Eliran. "Ephraim." *Map - Ephraim - BibleBento.Com*. **bit.ly/vwb-map-bb-ephraim**. Accessed 12 Aug. 2023.

Zank, Michael. "Exile & Return." *Jerusalem: The Holy City*. Boston University. **bit.ly/vwb-zank**. Accessed 17 Feb. 24.

IMAGE CREDITS

INTRODUCTION

- Photo of Soap Box Created by DALL·E 2024-01-10 19.13.44.
- All doodles and clip art (licensed).
- Photo of Person Digging with a Shovel (licensed).

CHAPTER 1: EVE

- Photo of Black Woman with Flowers in her Hair by Autumn Goodman on Unsplash.
- Background Floral Photo by Ehteshamul Haque Adit on Unsplash.
- Photo "Pillars of Creation (NIRCam Image)" by NASA, ESA, CSA, and STScI. Public Domain.
- Photo of hand tossing dirt by Kunj Parekh on Unsplash.
- Photo of Latrun Valley, Israel by Dmitry Mishin on Unsplash.
- Screenshots from BibleHub.com Hebrew Interlinear Bible. **biblehub.com/genesis/3-11.htm** and **biblehub.com/genesis/3-13.htm**. Fair use.
- Photo of Person Holding Plate of Figs (licensed).

CHAPTER 2: SARAH

- Photo of Older South Asian Woman Smiling by Loren Joseph on Unsplash.
- Coloured postcard of "Abraham's Oak" by Karimeh Abbud, circa 1925. Image is in the public domain in the United States.

CHAPTER 3: HAGAR

- Photo of Multiracial Pregnant Woman at Monahans Sandhills State Park by Matt Nelson on Unsplash.
- Photo of Pregnant Woman Performing Morning Exercises (licensed).
- Photo of Pilgrims on the al-Mas'aa Path (licensed).
- The Kaaba in Mecca, and the directions of the ritual walk during en:Hajj is an original drawing by Sureyya Aydin, 1992, first published in the educational book Inn i det ukjente, by NRK (Norwegian broadcasting corporation). Wikimedia Commons, licensed under CC BY-SA 3.0.* **https://en.m.wikipedia.org/wiki/File:Tavaf.jpg**.
- Photo of "View from Mount Sinai at sunrise. Beautiful mountain landscape in Egypt" (licensed).

CHAPTER 4: RACHEL & LEAH

- Photo of Two Women in White Dresses by Chalo Garcia on Unsplash.
- Photo of Sheep by Sam Carter on Unsplash.
- Photo of a Handshake by Ave Calvar on Unsplash.
- Photo of Group of Boys by Church of the King on Unsplash.
- "Family Tree of Jacob" by Laura Zielke.

* All Creative Commons Licenses are linked on page 180

CHAPTER 5: SHIPHRAH & PUAH

- Photo of Pregnant Woman Being Checked by Female Doula (licensed).
- Photo of a Water Channel with Boat in Egypt, with a Pyramid in the Background by Ruben Hanssen on Unsplash.
- Close-up of the Hieroglyphs Carved on an Ancient Wall in Egypt (licensed).
- Photo of Wall Mural in the Temple of Karnak by AXP Photography on Unsplash.
- Photo of Ancient Clay Tablet: "Birth of Sargon of Akkad." c. 2334-2279 BCE. Louvre Museum, Paris. Wikimedia Commons. Public Domain. bit.ly/vwb-wiki-sargon.
- Photo of the Ancient Temples in Luxor, Egypt (licensed).

CHAPTER 6: JOCHEBED & MIRIAM

- Photo of Mother with Three Children (licensed).
- Photo of Nile & Egyptian Desert Aesthetic by Jordi Orts Segalés on Unsplash.
- Photo of People Playing Tambourine at a Traditional Religious Festival (licensed).
- Photo of Merneptah Stele by Ovedc. "Kairo Museum Merenptah-Stele 01." Wikimedia Commons, 27 June 2010. Wikimedia Commons, licensed under CC BY-SA 3.0.* bit.ly/vwb-stele. Accessed 18 May 2024. Corrected to enhance detail.

CHAPTER 7: RAHAB

- Photo of Woman with Orange Hair on Bed by Kamaji Ogino on Pexels.
- Jericho photo by Valdemaras D. on Unsplash.
- Photo of Red Cord (licensed).

CHAPTER 8: SHEERAH

- Photo of Female Architect (licensed).
- Photo of Time in Spiral (licensed).
- Millennial woman using mobile phone sitting on top of desk with a cup of tea that says LIKE A BOSS (licensed).
- Photo of Woman with Hard Hat (licensed).
- Photo of Bayt 'Ur al-Tahta, Palestine by ילאכימ. 29 Mar. 2007. Wikimedia Commons, licensed under CC0 BY 1.0.* bit.ly/vwb-wiki-bayt.
- Photo of Matat Lookout in Bet-Horon, by ד:סוליצ רי'יבא ישיבכ רכייט Wikimedia Commons, licensed under CC BY 2.5.* bit.ly/vwb-siki-matat.
- Photo of Beit Horon from West Side by ןורוח תיב תוריכזמ. 9 Nov. 2017. Wikimedia Commons, licensed under CC0 BY 1.0.* bit.ly/vwb-beithoron.
- Photo of "The Triumphal Relief of Shoshenq I, depicting the god Amun-Re, near the Bubastite Portal at Karnak, Egypt" by Olaf Tausch. Wikimedia Commons, licensed under CC BY 3.0.* bit.ly/vwb-wiki-karnak.
- Screenshot of the heiroglyph found at the Temple of Karnak from *An Egyptian Hieroglyphic Dictionary* by Sir E. A. Wallis Budge, 1857-1934. bit.ly/vwb-budge.

CHAPTER 9: NAOMI, RUTH, & ORPAH

- Chapter Cover Photo "Out with My Girls" (licensed).
- Photo of Wheat Bushels in Basket by Laura James on Pexels.
- Map: Divided Kingdoms of Israel and Judah, ca. 9th Century BCE by Oldtidens_Israel_&_Judea.svg, derivative work: Richardprins (talk). Wikimedia Commons, licensed under CC BY-SA 3.0.* https://bit.ly/vwb-wiki-kingdoms.
- Photo of Ring by Jeremy Bishop on Unsplash.
- Photo of newborn baby boy by Jasmin Avakyants. Used with permission. ❤️

* All Creative Commons Licenses are linked on page 180

- Photo of Tree by Rocks in Israel by Milada Vigerova on Unsplash.
- Cornelis de Bruijn. Bethlehem. 1698, painting, 24.1 cm x 63.5 cm. Wikimedia Commons Public domain. bit.ly/vwb-wiki-bruijn. Accessed 29 Jun. 2024. Photo of artwork cropped to fit the page and color-corrected to bring out the details.

CHAPTER 10: DEBORAH

- Chapter Cover Photo of Woman under Palm Trees by Robert Stokoe on Pexels.
- Photo of Palm Tree by Levi Arnold on Unsplash.
- Map of 12 Tribes of Israel by 12 tribus de Israel.svg: Translated by Kordas12 staemme israels heb.svg: by user:יסוי12 staemme israels.png: by user:Janzderivative work Richardprins (talk). Wikimedia Commons, licensed under CC BY-SA 3.0.* bit.ly/vwb-wiki-12tribes.
- Photo of Jezreel Valley with Mt. Tabor in the distance (licensed).

CHAPTER 11: JAEL

- Chapter Cover Photo of Woman Near Tent by Art House Studio on Pexels.
- Photo of River Kishon ("Nesher") by Hanay. Wikimedia Commons, licensed under CC BY-SA 3.0.* bit.ly/vwb-wiki-kishon.
- Photo of Person Holding a Glass of Milk (licensed).
- Photo of Persian Rug by Sina Saadatmand on Unsplash.
- Photo of the Jezreel Valley by Joe Freeman. Wikimedia Commons, licensed under CC BY-SA 2.5.* bit.ly/vwb-wiki-jezreel.

CHAPTER 12: HANNAH

- Photo of Pregnant Woman Holding Blocks Spelling BOY by Alicia Zinn on Pexels.
- Tel Shiloh photo by Deror Avi. Wikimedia Commons, licensed under CC BY-SA 4.0.* bit.ly/vwb-wiki-shiloh.
- Photo of Woman Crying in Prayer by Katalin Salles on Unsplash.
- Photo of my adorable great-nephew (age 3) by Savannah Abercrombie. Used with permission. ❤️
- Image of 3-year-old Bovine. Generated by DALL·E. 2024-02-05.
- Image of a robe typical for a Middle Eastern child around 1000 BCE. Generated by DALL·E 2024-03-07 15.22.18.

CHAPTER 13: BATHSHEBA

- Photo Lifestyle Shower Moments of a Young Woman at Home (licensed).
- Photo of Soaps on Wash Cloth by Micheile Henderson on Unsplash.
- Photo of Two Men Drinking by Cottonbro Studio on Pexels.
- Photo of a "Temple of Solomon Model" by SalemOptix. Wikimedia Commons, licensed under CC BY-SA 4.0.* bit.ly/vwb-wiki-temple.
- Close-up photo of the Tel Dan Stele by לעי ר. "Close-up 3 - Tel Dan Inscription. 15 Jan. 2013, 19:17:32. Israel Museum, Jerusalem. Wikimedia Commons, licensed under CC BY-SA 3.0.* Unported license. bit.ly/vwb-wiki-teldan.

CHAPTER 14: JEHOSHEBA

- Photo of Woman and Young Boy by Bruno Nascimento on Unsplash.
- Photo of Black Woman Holding Magnifying Glass by Marten Newhall on Unsplash.
- Map: Divided Kingdoms of Israel and Judah, ca. 9th Century BCE by Oldtidens_Israel_&_Judea.svg, derivative work: Richardprins (talk). Wikimedia Commons, licensed under CC BY-SA 3.0.* bit.ly/vwb-wiki-kingdoms.

* All Creative Commons Licenses are linked on page 180

"The Genealogy of the Kings of Ancient Israel and Judah," is a derivative of the original image. Wikimedia Commons, licensed under CC BY-SA 3.0*. This image has been modified by re-centering the title, moving the legend, and reversing the horizontal direction of Pekehiah's succession for page fit. You can find the original image at **bit.ly/vwb-wiki-kings**.

- Photo of Woman with Finger on Lips by Kristina Flour on Unsplash.
- Photo of Boy Wearing Crown by Valario Davis on Unsplash.
- Photo of Screaming Woman (licensed).
- Photo of "Samaria, the Capital of the Kingdom of Israel in Ancient Times - Today an Archaeological Site" by Daniel Ventura. 4 Apr. 2007. Own work. Wikimedia Commons, licensed under CC BY-SA 3.0.* Unported license. **bit.ly/vwb-wiki-samaria**.

CHAPTER 15: HULDAH

- Photo of Black Woman at Podium by Nkululeko Mabena on Unsplash.
- Photo of "Old Coins Half 1/2 Israel Sheqel - Sheqalim Israeli Coin Lion of Judah" used with permission by Antique Items @matanshalom100 on eBay. Visit the store here: **ebay.com/str/worldcoins**.
- "The Second Part of the All Souls Deuteronomy, Containing the Decalogue" by Author unknown, photograph by Shai Halevi - **deadseascrolls.org.il/explore-the-archive/image/B-298337**, Public Domain, **bit.ly/vwb-wiki-4q41**.
- Photo of Large Crowd of People by CHUTTERSNAP on Unsplash.

CHAPTER 16: VASHTI

- Photo of Young Woman Wearing a Tiara by Albany Capture on Unsplash.
- Photo of "Empress Crown" by Van Cleef & Arpels. Wikimedia Commons, licensed under CC BY-SA 4.0.* International License. **bit.ly/vwb-wiki-crown**. Modified by color correction and background removal by Laura Zielke.
- Photo of "Darius Palace" by Babak Sedighi. September 7, 2009. UNESCO World Heritage Centre, **whc.unesco.org/en/documents/137122**. Copyright ICCHTO. Licensed under Nomination File (non-exclusive cession of rights: yes) with the condition of use requiring attribution and no derivatives.
- Photo of "Human-headed Aladlammu in Darius palace in Susa" by Alemazi. Wikimedia Commons, licensed under CC BY-SA 4.0.* **bit.ly/vwb-wiki-aladlammu.**
- Photo of "Frieze of Griffins, circa 510 BCE, Apadana, west courtyard of the palace, Susa, Iran" by Wikimedia Commons user Carole Raddato. Wikimedia Commons, licensed under CC BY-SA 2.0.* **bit.ly/vwb-griffins**.
- Photo of "Immortels - dynamosquito" by Dynamosquito. Wikimedia Commons, licensed under CC BY-SA 4.0.* **bit.ly/vwb-wiki-immortels**.

CHAPTER 17: ESTHER

- Photo of Woman Dancing on Beach by "seb" on Unsplash.
- Photo of Stylish Man and Woman with Retro Bike (licensed).
- Photo of Banquet Table by Pablo Lancaster Jones on Pexels.
- Photo of Hand Holding Red Rose (licensed); Golden Scepter (licensed).
- Photo of Purim Party Supplies (licensed).
- Collage of Traditional Middle Eastern or Arab Dish (licensed).
- Photo of Horemheb's ring at the Louvre Museum. Wikimedia Commons, licensed under CC 1.0.* **bit.ly/vwb-wiki-signet**.
- Photo of Five Children in Costume Headed to a Purim Carnival (licensed).

All Creative Commons Licenses are linked on page 180

CHAPTER 18: CONCLUSION

📷 Photo of Woman Reading Bible by Joel Muniz on Unsplash.
📷 Photos of women are documented in their respective chapters.

CREATIVE COMMONS LICENSE LINKS:

🔗 https://creativecommons.org/licenses/by-sa/1.0/
🔗 https://creativecommons.org/licenses/by-sa/2.0/
🔗 https://creativecommons.org/licenses/by-sa/2.5/
🔗 https://creativecommons.org/licenses/by-sa/3.0/
🔗 https://creativecommons.org/licenses/by-sa/4.0/

🗝 5 KEYS TO RESPONSIBLE BIBLE INTERPRETATION

Responsible Bible interpretation is essential for understanding Scripture in a meaningful and accurate way. Here are five key principles to guide your study as you commit to responsible interpretation:

1. Context Matters
Always consider the historical, cultural, and literary context of a passage. Understanding the time, place, and circumstances in which a text was written helps to grasp its intended meaning.

2. Genre Recognition
The Bible contains various literary genres, including poetry, narrative, prophecy, and epistles. Recognizing the genre helps to interpret the text appropriately, as different genres have different rules for interpretation.

3. Scripture Interprets Scripture
Use other parts of the Bible to help interpret challenging passages. The Bible often provides clarification or further insight into its own teachings, allowing for a more cohesive understanding.

4. Authorial Intent
Strive to understand what the original author intended to communicate to the original audience. This involves studying the language, customs, and worldview of the time to avoid imposing modern ideas onto ancient texts.

5. Application with Integrity
Apply the lessons and teachings of the Bible to modern life in a way that is faithful to its original meaning. Be cautious of over-allegorizing or making the text say something it doesn't, ensuring that applications are rooted in the text's true intent.

KEYWORD INDEX

ABOUT THE AUTHOR

Laura L. Zielke (ZELL-kee) has been offering fresh perspectives in the world of biblical studies through her thoughtful and accessible approach to Scripture for nearly 40 years.

As the oldest daughter of a Southern Baptist pastor, Laura's upbringing grounded her in Scripture and shaped her lifelong commitment to learning and teaching God's Word. From birth, Laura's love for the Bible was nurtured by her parents. With her mom as her first (and most frequent) Sunday School teacher and her dad as pastor, she easily had three to four hours a week of solid Bible teaching until she left for college at the age of 17.

It was from this solid foundation she went on to earn a Bachelor of Arts in Religion from California Baptist University (formerly California Baptist College). It was there she fell in love with New Testament Greek and enjoyed the distinction of being the first female Greek tutor. At graduation, she was honored with the *Outstanding Senior Woman in the Department of Religion Award* and the *American Bible Society's Biblical Greek Award*.

Photos top to bottom; left to right: Laura facilitating a college study group as Greek tutor; Graduating class of Religion Majors (college); Photo from the first night of the Complementary Education Program at MBTS; Laura receiving her Master of Divinity Degree; The only two women to receive an MDiv in Laura's graduating class at MBTS.

After college, Laura was accepted into an honors program at Midwestern Baptist Theological Seminary which afforded her the opportunity to bypass introductory courses (since she had majored in Religion), and spend the next three years in advanced courses where she focused on Biblical Studies, Greek, and Archaeology.

From Midwestern, she graduated *summa cum laude* with a Master of Divinity degree and received two prestigious awards: *The Wornall Road Baptist Church Award in Theological Field Education* for excellence in ministry under supervision, and the *Wanda J. Keetly Award* for being an outstanding graduate who demonstrated both excellence in the area of Biblical Studies and an interest in continued scholarship and ministry.

Laura's passion for equipping and elevating women in the church was shaped by her unique experiences as the only female religion major in her graduating class at Cal Baptist and as one of just two women to earn an MDiv in her graduating class at Midwestern.

1. Seated on the steps of the Temple Mount at the Southern Wall Archaeological Park, Jerusalem; 2. "Riding" a camel in the Holy Land near the Dead Sea; 3. Enjoying every second at Qumran, an ancient community dedicated to preserving the written Word. It was in these caves that the Dead Sea Scrolls were discovered between 1946 and 1956. Cave 4 (behind me) yielded the largest collection of manuscripts at the site and some of the oldest manuscripts of books in the Hebrew Bible ever found (so far!).

One memorable experience she had in college led her to pioneer a life-changing program in seminary. Due to the demographics in her college major, Laura was regularly teamed up with married men for group projects. Once, while waiting for a group member to return home, Laura spent time with his wife and learned she felt like she was being left behind while her husband advanced in his knowledge of the Bible and theological studies.

This encounter highlighted a systemic issue: the training of one spouse for ministry while completely neglecting their partner. These partners, almost exclusively women, were often busy caring for their babies and young children and/or working full-time jobs to support their husbands' education. This disconnect often led to feelings of isolation and stagnation. The problem was even more pronounced in seminary.

In response to this great need, Laura established a new, groundbreaking program at her seminary aimed exclusively at educating student spouses (99% women). The "Complementary Education Program" was designed not only to teach Bible basics, key theological concepts, and training for ministry but also to provide them with an opportunity to enjoy one guest lecture per course from the same professors their husbands had. This approach aimed to foster a more inclusive educational journey, enrich their conversations with a common vocabulary about biblical topics, and deepen their spiritual and intellectual partnership.

The 2-year program culminated in a special graduation ceremony exclusively for these spouses, recognizing their achievement with an official Certificate in Ministry from the seminary. Due to its success, the program soon expanded to all six Southern Baptist seminaries, significantly impacting the seminary community nationwide.

Since seminary, Laura has served in a variety of roles including youth minister, lay pastor, small group facilitator, Sunday School teacher, and board member. She also taught Greek and New Testament to high school students at a Classical Christian School before stepping away to home educate her only child from the second grade through high school. During their home-schooling journey, Laura taught a variety of enrichment courses to middle school and high school students, as well as a college-level course for the moms on hermeneutics (how to study the Bible).

More recently, Laura led an adult Sunday School class on a four-year journey verse-by-verse through the *Gospel of Mark*, which she translated from the original Greek. This endeavor continued into the *Acts of the Apostles*.

Advocating for responsible Bible study has been a consistent thread throughout Laura's career. She continues to fact-check sermons, challenge false assumptions, and call out bad theology—especially Christian Nationalism. She is convinced that many of the problems we are dealing with in the church today are due to rushed, incomplete exegesis and an over-reliance on someone else's unverified conclusions. Laura

consistently encourages people of faith to start with what the Scripture actually says, and then from there, use a variety of tools and resources to dig into the historical and cultural contexts to understand the meaning.

In her debut book, *Valiant Women of the Bible, Volume 1: From Eve to Esther*, Laura moves the narratives of biblical women out of the shadows into the light, offering deep insights in a way that is educational, inspiring, and accessible to the average reader. This book is the first in a series designed to reclaim the stories of influential women from the Bible.

As Laura prepares to explore the lives of women in the New Testament in her upcoming second volume, she continues to inspire and educate. Her work connects deeply with readers, encouraging them to see the transformative power of faith and perseverance in their own lives and then to pass it on. ✦

Couple selfie at Yellowstone National Park, 2024

Laura has been happily married to John Zielke for 28 years. They met on America Online in the mid-90s, and never looked back. Their 22-year old is a skilled video editor and gifted photographer. Although John and Laura both hail from the west coast, they have called North Carolina home for more than 20 years. As a family, they prefer driving to flying, and have driven coast to coast many times.

DID YOU ENJOY THE BOOK?

If so, I would be truly grateful if you could take a moment to share your thoughts in a brief review on **Amazon.com, GoodReads.com**, or your favorite online bookstore. Your feedback not only helps other readers discover the book but also supports my work. Thank you so much for your time and support!

BONUS CONTENT & ERRATA:

https://valiantwomenofthebible/bonus
https://valiantwomenofthebible.com/errata

JOIN THE VALIANT COMMUNITY™ ON MIGHTY NETWORKS!

https://valiantwomenofthebible.com/community

To book Laura Zielke as a speaker for your event, please reach out via email at **info@laurazielke.com**, or leave a detailed voice message at 336-497-1447.

One QR Code to Rule Them All! Scan or visit here to connect: **https://laurazielke.com/connect**

NOTES & REFLECTIONS

Laura L. Zielke is a respected Bible teacher, author, and speaker, known for her interdisciplinary approach to Bible interpretation and engaging teaching style. Beloved by her students, she excels at making complex concepts easy to understand and uncovering insights that often go unnoticed.

With a passion for responsible Bible interpretation, Laura guides readers in uncovering the rich, often overlooked stories of women in the Bible.

Her work empowers individuals to engage deeply with their faith and find fresh insights in ancient texts.

To connect with Laura L. Zielke, scan the QR code or visit: laurazielke.com/connect

www.ingramcontent.com/pod-product-compliance
Lightning Source LLC
Chambersburg PA
CBHW051147120626
46547CB00012B/975